Policing Our Own

By Timothy Trull

One of the most life changing moments of my existence was around 2007 when I was in Fulton, Missouri attending a class at Fulton College. I was in town, going to a restaurant, when I observed a heavy set, African American woman in one of those thin, faded flowery dresses you only see in the South, get out of the passenger's side of the older modeled car she was in, walk over to a young man with pants hanging down and his underwear showing on the sidewalk, and stated very loud "you are what is wrong with Black people. You make us all look bad. Pull up your pants. What is wrong with you. You look like a pimp thug. You are not in prison." She then got back in the car and kept going. The young man pulled up his pants, tightened his belt, and looked down. I never knew if that was his mother or who the woman was, but it was impressive. That is what we need more of in the world, not just in the black communities but in every community. We, human beings, have the responsibility to Police others. We are our brother's keeper.

### *Previous works by the Author:*

As the Baptist Church Goes, There Goes America

The Plumbline

Untempered Mortar: A Time for Moral Leaders

Small Cracks: The Resurgence of Urim and Thummim

America is the Moral Authority

## Introduction

When the first Spaniards came to America, they were looking for gold. When they could not find gold, they took Indians as slaves back to Europe, and sold them to the highest bidder. Some European's who stayed in America, kept Indians as slaves themselves. However, many of the Indians died on ships being transported back to Europe. At the time, there were many Europeans who wanted to come to America. Some were willing to enslave themselves for transport to America, and others were just kidnapped for sell in America. Thus was the beginning of slave trade in America. European's who settled in America were primarily farmers, and had to make a living off the land. Slaves and indentured servants were the cheapest means of having labor for these struggling farmers. The slave trade by the 1600's was booming in Africa. Black people made good slaves as they could be transported without dying on ships as quickly as the Indian's did, and they were not like white indentured servants, who had to be freed after so many years. The norm became that African men, women and children were enslaved in Africa, brought to America, and became slaves or indentured servants to European peoples who had come to America. Some slaves had destinies to become great men, such as Titus Cornelius, also known as Colonel Tye, who was a slave born in New Jersey, with ancestry from Africa. Colonel Tye was one of the most effective guerrilla leaders opposing the American Revolutionary forces in central New Jersey. He ran away from his master in November 1775, and joined the British Militia to fight against the American Revolutionaries. The British paid him and other black runaway slaves to destabilize the American region, and to fight against George Washington

.

and his men.  He provided substantial aid to the British during the Revolutionary War, and helped British forces withstand a 1779 siege during the winter by American forces led by General George Washington. In September 1780, Colonel Tye raided the home of Revolutionary War Captain Joshua Huddy, and was injured by a musket ball that passed through his wrist.  He soon thereafter developed tetanus, and died.  After the American's won the war, slavery continued and farms grew.  Cotton became king, and the primary labor supply for these farms was slaves.  African slave labor became the normal way of life, especially in the South, as farms grew, and men knew no different.  However, slaves did not always work willingly.  Many slaves worked slow, and there were many revolts, including in 1663 a revolt in Glouchester County, Virginia where white indentured servants conspired with black slaves to revolt to obtain their freedom.

In mainstream society, there were few men or women speaking up and saying slavery was wrong, because the majority of the citizens thought slavery a "necessary evil."  We European's at that time, failed to Police our own.  However, in the mid 1800's, men and women started speaking out against slavery, and by the 1860's, the country was divided.  To hold a man in bondage was without a doubt wrong, as the Bible stated that all men are equal in the eyes of God, and because it was a known fact that all men have a soul, and deserve the freedom to find life, liberty , and the pursuit of happiness.  Because of these people who were willing to speak up against the evils of slavery, the United States went to war.  While arguments loom that there are varying reasons for the Civil War, the fundamental disagreement between the newly formed Confederate States of America and the established United States of America was over the issue of slavery, and Abraham

Lincoln's leadership and effort to abolish it.  Many good men from both sides of the American Civil War ended their time on this earth fighting in this battle of seemingly good against evil.  Following the Civil War and the reunification of the United States, slavery was abolished, and African American's and white indentured servants, were freed in the US if they wanted to stay, or allowed to go back to Africa or wherever else they were from if they wanted.  The rights of the African American's who remained in the US continued to slowly, and sometimes painfully, grow through the 1900's, and culminated in 2008 when the first American African American President was elected.  At this point, many African American people felt they were truly free, and many white people were proud of how far we had come to settle racial differences.  However, others wanted more.  Some African American's harbored hatred over how their ancestors were brought over as slaves from Africa.  Some African American's still harbor this hate in their heart, and dream of a day of revenge against the descendants of these "white imperialists," some of whom they mistakenly confuse with the descendants of initial indentured servants.  Their hatred and seeking of revenge is however, non-Biblical, and the lack of forgiveness causes hate in their hearts.

The Bible clearly states in Ezekiel 18:20 that "the one who sins is the one who will die.  The child will not share the guilt of the parent, nor will the parent share the guilt of the child."  However, a large group of African American's, mainly from Chicago, want to use the slavery issue from the early part of American history, as a rallying call to African American's to take over the country, like America is a 3rd world country with 3rd rate citizens.  Luckily, the forefathers of our country were smart enough to envision the day when a man might become President, and deem himself as more of a man than a mere mortal, and attempt to take power as an emperor. In the Christian sense of seeking forgiveness, many American's, wanted to overlook these Chicago individuals, and prayed they would find forgiveness as only Jesus can give. Many just pray for this un-Godly time to pass, so we can replace these Satan led people with God inspired individuals. Unfortunately, these same people soon became ensnared in a racial time bomb. For example, if a white person stated that African American men should follow the laws of the authorities over them, then they (the white people) were considered racist. Many men became labelled as racist, who had never even considered race an issue, and were themselves a victim of racism. The question arises, if a group of white men and women went through Ferguson, Missouri, broke into the liquor store to steal all the liquor, got liquored up, and then went through Ferguson and burned the town down, they would be called an extremist hate group and militia. They would be put in the Southern Poverty Law Centers list of hate crime people, and be on every Federal Bureau of Investigation (FBI) and National Security Administration (NSA) watch list in the country. However, African American's, burned down towns, and no one Policed them because if you did you were called a racist.

Well, I dispute it and I am tired of it. My name is Tim Trull. I am a white American, but I have some Native American blood. My ancestors were poorer that dirt, and became indentured servants to step foot in America, and we are not smart or rich. My ancestors farmed the land and worked in mills and factories and manufacturing plants so as to have money to eat. We (the Trull family) probably could not have planned to bring a slave from South Carolina, much less from Africa. So as you attack me as being racist, and as a hate crime because I am calling this modern generation of black people from Chicago racist, know this. I am not racist, and am just tired. I am tired of the black privilege being given to black people because of the sins of my supposed fathers. I cannot help what happened in 1835, but I can help what is happening today, and I am scared for my country and my family. As a white person looking out today, it appears that African American people are trying to make Washington, DC more and more like North Korea, with a supreme leader and an inner circle of people who will protect the supreme leader, and no one is stepping in to Police it. When you speak against a black man who is breaking the law or attacking a Police Officer, you become a racist. Police have to watch arresting black people for any crimes because of the word "racist." The steps we have made in the US, for equality, and peace between the races are being torn down because of the "black lives matter" campaign. No other lives matter. Only "black lives matter." That is the most racist thing I have ever heard, as I hear daily about white Police Officers being shot and killed, and white families being killed by black people. The arguments you keep hearing for these black people killing whites is "they are just victims." "The black kid would not have killed the white family if his mother was not on crack, and he had a better chance with life." I was not smart, but took my chance to make something with my life by joining the Marine Corps. Many black people are smarter than I am, and many have worked harder to get through this life than even I have. This modern "crack mother" reasoning to let black killers free is ridiculous. It is an insult to black people who follow the laws and just want to be left alone to pursue life, liberty, and the pursuit of happiness. My Bible says the same thing that theirs does. Thou shalt not kill. Thou shalt not steal. Honor thy mother and father. Thou shalt obey the government appointed over you. This Bible that I am quoting, that many people have begun to call useless or out of date, is the rock that our foundation rests upon, for blacks, whites, Asians, Hispanics, and everyone else who calls America home. America is being destroyed because all races are ignoring the tenants of our creator. Our government is being taken over by street thugs, with no caring about the common man. Call me racist. It is a lie, and will not be the only one you say today. The liberal left has no moral values, because they left their code of moral values their mother tried to teach them about, so they could earn the votes of drug dealers and welfare recipients. We, the United States of America, are becoming what thousands of men fought in wars to keep us from becoming; a Communist Nation. I don't want to see the United States of America become North Korea or worse.

## Chapter (1) The Apes

*"When I was in the Marine Corps, I felt like everyone was always trying to find something wrong with you. Senior Marines and even Junior Marines would always say things like fix your cover, or you have a string on your uniform, or that is yes sir or yes mam to you. To me, who is definitely not a perfectionist, it was annoying. But, it kept me looking. I hated to have someone say something to me to correct me so much to where I looked at my uniform every day to make sure it looked right, kept my boots spit shined, and walked a straight line. I even got to where I saluted everyone that was not in uniform, for fear I would miss saluting someone of higher rank."* As I started reading the Bible every day, and knowing what God wanted from me, I started acting the same way. I just needed to know.

My son, when he was eight years old, heard someone talking about how man may have evolved from apes. In fact, he heard this both on television and at school, against our teaching at home that man was created by God, as stated in Genesis. He said, "dad, if we evolved from apes like they say at school, why are there still apes?" While I as a Judeo-Christian never really believed we had evolved from apes, I stopped for a minute and thought, "hey, here is a rational statement. If we evolved from apes, why are there still apes?" So, from then on, every time I heard some overeducated argument for the human evolution of man from apes, I thought my 8 year old son's thoughts in my mind, "yeah, why are there still apes." We all (Judeo-Christians) believe God created the heavens and the earth, mankind, angels, animals, insects, and everything else; so in our mind the evolution theory is eternally flawed. However, the evolution of man is a planned television topic or agenda, and one that is more likely seen than anything on God and his plan for the world. "Bob," is the best name I could come up with for the guy that is programming television stations to change our viewpoints on everything from gay marriage to transvestite men using women's restrooms, and wants me not to believe in the Bible anymore, but to believe in man's version of evolution. Bob is really Satan, or his agent, but I had rather call him Bob. Bob made billions of dollars off the currency markets in London, destroying the little guy so he can become rich and rule the world and claim to be an atheist. So, just anytime I mention Bob, know I am really talking about Satan, who is the father of all lies, a murderer, and wants us all to be on his agenda against God's will, and against the rule of Jesus Christ in our lives. Bob is fully aligned with Russia, Iran, Syria, and North Korea. Bob, on his website, when you look up his name, states he is an atheist. However, he believes in God, and he knows the end is nearing.

Bob has been a thorn in the side, so to say, of human civilizations since before Adam and Eve.   Thus, planned television and media has a direction planned by Bob, and we sheep are led in its direction daily, if we choose to watch it.  We ignore the Bible, and depend on Bob to tell us how to live our lives, through entertaining Hollywood movies.  However, who plans these movies, television shows, and the topics and direction it goes in.  It increasingly takes the direction that Bob (or Satan) wants the world to take.  He is doing his work through men who think they are just worldly, and are conforming to what they perceive the world should believe. These individuals call themselves "left wing," or "human rights activists."  However, they are not really caring for anyone else, and are very selfish for their own needs, making six figure salaries in the name of "progressive" news.  They are not news analysts, because as we all know, television news is severely lacking of any analytical thought.   So, who is controlling this television reporting at the highest levels, and telling the station chiefs which direction to take, such as informing all people that white Police Officers are racist?   Who is behind this?  The answer is "Bob."

Job 1: 6 "Now there was a day when the sons of God came to present themselves before the Lord, and Satan came also among them.  And the Lord said to Satan, whence comest thou? Then Satan answered the Lord and said, From going to and fro in the earth, and from walking up and down in it.  And the Lord said to Satan. Hast thou considered my servant Job, that there is none like him in the earth, a perfect and an upright man, one that feareth God, and escheweth evil?  Then Satan answered the Lord, and said, Doth Job fear God for nought?  Hast not thou made an hedge about him, and about his house, and about all that he hath on every side?  Thou hast blessed the work of his hands, and his substance is increased in the land."

## Chapter (2) Evolution

*Matthew 21:12   Jesus entered the temple and drove out all those who were buying and selling in the temple, and overturned the tables of the money changers and the seats of those who were selling doves.  He said to them, "It is written my house shall be called a house of prayer, but you are making it a robbers den."*

All of us Judeo-Christians were taken aback by the shooting that took place in Ferguson, Missouri by a white Police Officer of an unarmed, black male.  No one wanted to see anyone get shot, and I am sure the Police Officer who shot Michael Brown has played this over and over in his mind on how a different outcome could have come about.  However, immediately following the shooting, African American's, many hired from Bob's office in Chicago, took to the street demanding justice be done to the Police Officer.  When the facts came out that the Police Officer had shot the subject to protect his own life, and that the subject had in fact strong armed stolen cigars from a store clerk minutes earlier, it changed nothing.  The same select African American's still marched to the street and demanded "pretend" justice from the white Police Officer, under orders to march from their Chicago office, and to get African American's from Ferguson and the surrounding area to join in.  I say "pretend justice" because justice was served from a thoughtful and tearful jury of 12 private citizens who had seen all the evidence and did not charge the Police Officer with a crime; but the individuals protesting from Chicago wanted more.  These men and women wanted a lynching, like white people used to have in Alabama and other Southern States against a black man accused of a crime. This lynching agenda was supported and televised in its entirety by four out of five of the largest networks in the United States. White police officers do not target black men to arrest and shoot. They target crime, look for reasonable suspicion, and need probable cause to make an arrest. However, Bob doesn't care about the truth, because it does not demand anarchy and division. Bob's statement was that even though Mr. Brown may have stolen cigars, and was attacking the Police Officer and even reaching into his Police Car trying to take the Officers weapon, that the Police Officer had no right to defend himself, because he was a white Police Officer and the subject was black. The truth was that if it was a white subject who had strong armed stolen a box of cigars, and then assaulted a black Police Officer sitting in his cruiser, and the black Police Officer would have shot the white subject, that it would not have even made the local news. I say this because of the story of a white teenager (Zachary Hammond) who was shot in the back in Seneca, South Carolina in August, 2015 by a seasoned white Police Officer, and it did not even make the news until a huge amount of people noticed the disparity. CNN, NBC, ABC, CBS seemingly went out of their way toward ignoring the story until they were called on the carpet by the masses. Fox News was the only television station that seemingly gave it even a mention. Bob just wanted it to go away. There was a story line that a reporter like Lois Lane in Superman would have loved to have got her hands on. The story that the Police Department came out with was that Zachary was shot while trying to hit a known Police Lieutenant with his car. However, there was evidence to dispute this statement, such as he was shot in the back. This shooting was contradictory to Police statements, but there are no protests, and the television networks are not really discussing this. Bob is overly quiet in seeking justice for the Hammond family. While the family demanded answers, and buried the dead teen, there was no looting of the Seneca Wal-Mart for Zachary. There were no masses from Chicago, Illinois that travelled to Seneca, South Carolina and paid $13 an hour to protest the kid being killed, and breaking into the Seneca liquor store. The normal talking heads from Chicago, who had stirred trouble in Ferguson, Missouri and Baltimore, Maryland were eerily quiet. Thus, it became apparent that these people, the protestors, did not care if whites or other races were killed during a bad interrogation or traffic stop by Police; just if African American's were. Thus, we have the double standard of racism, like we had at the beginning of Nazi Germany when the Nazi's slowly started moving toward taking property away from Jewish people and the normal German people did nothing. We American's must remember history, and not to allow these people from Chicago, who are amassing because of a wealthy, billionaire anarchist, to attack the America that was built for individual freedom, liberty, and the pursuit of happiness. And, we need to get a name of the group who is pulling together to create the disparity in the open, so as to understand who is behind this "agenda driven news." Who is Satan supporting? The best name, and the name that fits these individual's from Chicago, is Communists, supported by the Russian KGB, however they are led out of believe it or not, the old Hungary. And, as you dispute this, look who was handing out signs in Ferguson, a Communist Party.

Chapter 3 "Bob, the Media Mogul"

*"On August 22, 2015, three young men on a train in France heard the unmistakable sound of rounds being loaded in a weapon inside of a bathroom on a train. When the shooter began to come out, with a loaded AK-47 and a knife, these three men fought the man, and detained him until he could be arrested. Their actions saved many innocent lives. One of the individuals, a Specialist in the Oregon National Guard, received the Soldiers Medal."*

In 2015, the shooting of a young black man that was killed by a Police Officer while allegedly trying to take his gun, made national news (CBS, NBC, ABC, CNN, FOX), and the normal Communists showed up bused in from Chicago, Illinois, pretending to care for freedom and the black people, while they were being paid $13 an hour from a billionaire that is supposed to represent the best interests of African American's. Following this acquittal, from where they tried to charge the Police Officer in front of a Grand Jury, I am watching television and it appears I am watching something like out of the movie "Planet of the Apes." African American men (who mainly were not from Ferguson, Missouri) are running down the streets in Ferguson, Missouri, breaking and entering a liquor store first by the masses, drinking bottles of stolen liquor, and then turning over cars, looting, burning buildings including a Papa Johns Pizza….they were no longer human beings with a mind and conscience of right and wrong; they were animals with only the intention of destruction for anyone or anything that got in their way. It looked just like the scene off the Planet of the apes when Zeus turns over cars and is on the bridge attacking the military. In fact, I would say that Zeus was giving more conscience thought to who he attacked than the mob in

Ferguson did. However, none of this activity happened in Seneca, South Carolina for the young white man (Zachary Hammonds) that was killed, and the media did not try to hype it up, to create such. Thus, I started thinking. Maybe we did not evolve from apes, but maybe we are evolving into apes. Maybe Bob's agenda was for us to turn into animals just like Apes, with no real conscience of right and wrong. This would be also in line with Satan's plan since the beginning of time. Maybe Satan did not like when God gave men a conscience, as then they would be like the Angels, knowing right from wrong, as discussed at the tree of the knowledge of good and evil. Thus, I started doing a little research, and I believe I came closer to understanding Darwin's thinking. Apes travel, hunt, have sex, and think in groups. Many of us humans are the same way, as we have no independent thoughts left. Turn on the large television networks after a major event, and there is no longer any independent thinking. They (Bob) all speak the same direction now, as if it is all controlled by a Communist Gestapo. You turn on CNN, NBC, CBS, and ABC and they sell homosexuality as the greatest deal of the future, black people are still enslaved, and that Obama Health Care will save us all and be the greatest deal in the world ever. Fox News tries to give a better picture of the news, but even their statistics and "special topics" speakers are sometimes overly biased. The media rarely gives an analysis of the good points and bad points anymore, so that "we the people" can formulate a reasonable decision of what is right and wrong. The reason is that our government at the highest levels now no longer cares about "we the people," and the television stations are a reflection of our government. Rarely are statistics discussed anymore, and when they are they are skewed in an unfair manner, to support the argument. And, when we American people call bullshit, such as during the Iran deal, we are sold on the agenda like a life insurance salesman who won't take "no" for an answer, in a demeaning way that is like "you just don't get it." No one helps us get it. It is all agenda based reporting. The days of real analysis, such as was on CBS 60 Minutes before they were taken over by "Bob," is gone. They (all networks) sell their news and/or agendas with a multi-level styled marketing campaign, like they are pitching a get rich, multi-layered marketing scheme. "Don't worry about the products we sell, just get people under you to sell the product, and recruit people to buy into the organization, and you will become rich." It is like some man, "Bob," calls the big four liberal networks and says, "today let's put as much as possible on the news about how racist all white people, and especially white Police Officers are." Then, as African Americans take to the street and are running and burning buildings, the only station that is saying this is wrong is Fox News, while the other four networks are "justifying" the African American criminal activity. The newspaper can put an African American in the newspaper to argue why "Black Lives Matter," but when a white person writes an article in the Miami Herald that "All Lives Matter," he is deemed racist. Then they put a panel of women on ABC, and let them talk around the table, and their viewpoints always are in line with Bob's viewpoint, unless they put someone on there that appears "crazy" or "nutty", so we feel crazy if we oppose something. The media uses psychology to change the points of view of weak American's who watch. It is the same way that Judeo-Christians are portrayed in Hollywood movies, making us look crazy so no one would want to be like us. The cool guys are no longer John Wayne, Sam Elliott, or Clint Eastwood...they are Little Wayne, Spike Lee, or Charlie Sheen, or someone so evil. What is evil is good, and what is good is crazy or nutty. This

Hollywood agenda against Judeo-Christians is well thought out, planned, and scripted, just like the Chinese and North Korean's do with their television stations.

We have fought against Communism in the past. Dozens of statues exist throughout Washington, DC showing the names of men and women who died to protect our country from Communism. Today, modern American news organizations and social groups are embracing Communism, for some strange, lazy, un-American reason. Freedom of thought just like freedom of religion, are under attack. The newspaper reporters who are seeking "truth," and who want to uncover the big story, no longer exist. They are afraid of Bob, and his money. Men and women in journalism rarely have any intestinal fortitude or creative spirit, and when they do, they are attacked. In fact, it is my premise that the upper tiers of Washington, DC and Chicago politics are trying to make Washington, DC look more like Beijing and Pyongyang, and less like America. We have taken down our American flags, Confederate statues and memorials, and other flags which symbolize the history this country has gone through. The being that we are as a country was not free, and the memorials represent the best and worst of what made us who we are. When the people embrace Communism, and the lack of individuality of speech, they are embracing giving away a lot of individual rights, some of which have already been taken away. Freedom of the press is today almost an anomaly, due to the fear of being called "racist" or "against feminism," or a "homophobe." It was only eight years ago that the Pentagon was discharging Soldiers when they were gay, stating they had "mental problems." It was only eight years ago, that we were encouraging females to enter professions that they could use their feminism and motherly traits as assets, such as teaching or nursing. A man is a man. A woman is a woman. God made us different, and Bob wants us to believe otherwise, as if we were all "Pat" as he/she used to be played on Saturday Night Live. That was the funniest skit, trying to figure out if he/she was a he or a she. Today, that skit is anti-transvestite. Fast forward eight short years of Bob inspired media, and we are discussing having transvestites join the military, and displaying "gay pride" on the White House. The Bible, the rock that our country is built on, is never mentioned. God's will is never sought. Decisions about our country, and that could impact the world, are made without seeking God's will. People in Washington, DC make statements like "well transvestites should be allowed to choose whichever bathroom they feel most comfortable is." Never care about the rights of young girls and other children who use these restrooms beside a man dressed up pretending to be a woman; just care about the transvestite. People never disagree, and instead offer suggestive reasoning why Bob's opinion is right. There are no preachers on television stating "thou shalt not kill," or "thou shalt not steal," or "thou shalt obey the government that is appointed over you," as written in the Bible. Instead, there are just comments like "well, these African American men are upset over Michael Brown being unjustly shot," and deserve a time to let off steam. What did Papa John's Pizza in Ferguson, Missouri do to deserve to be burnt down? And, why was the first place broken into the liquor store, so they could all get drunk and party while they tore up a city. Why, because that is in line with Bob's desire. Liquor helps cover the conscience as decisions are made. Reporters make this justification statement for destruction on television even after a jury of 12 private citizens made a decision that the Police Officer was justified in shooting Michael Brown. In fact, the group from Chicago wanted to make such a scene on television, to where the next time there was a trial involving a Police Officer, the "jury" would remember the rioting that the Chicago group did, and influence their decision. If you fast forward to the 2015 trial of Officer Kerrick in Charlotte, NC who shot an African American male who charged at him after Officer Kerrick was called to a breaking-and-entering in progress call, it was the same thing. The Chicago based protestors travelling south to Charlotte, NC to infiltrate the Democratic masses. To the credit of the Charlotte, NC Police Department, they were prepared and handled them well.

## Chapter (4) Confusion

*Following the Revolutionary War, Congress wanted George Washington to serve as President for life. He was asked to be a new type of monarchy, but he turned it down as it was against what he had been fighting for. He wanted a government "by the people, for the people. " What he built, stood for 232 years, before the destruction began.*

In my mind, it is with a high probability that "Bob" is based in Chicago, but his or her face has still not been uncovered. We know he is a being that roams the earth, and causes destruction where he may. He is likely a billionaire, who makes his money destroying currency markets around the world. Bob's media contacts and money put the current President and his administration in office. In fact, it is with a high degree of confidence that I state the current President would not be in office if Bob had not arranged for a lot of corruption in the polls and voting places. Bob is a master at lying and deception.

Likewise, Bob will work diligently to put the next President in office, through confusion and the introduction of candidates that should be talk show hosts, instead of the leader of the free world.  George Washington, Abraham Lincoln, Franklin Roosevelt...real servant leaders who paid the price for leadership, are being replaced by the highest bidder and the most politically savvy person, who can lead the government the way Bob wants.  Jesus washed the feet of his disciples, and would not lead those who would not let him.  George Washington turned down being the "King" of America.  However, today, anyone can become President for the right price and connections to Bob; integrity, moral values, and servant leadership skills are not included for the price.  A knowledge of the Bible and of right and wrong are definitely not included.  We the people no longer deserve a moral President.

During the Ferguson riots, other news stations had commentators they got from somewhere who were all agreeing with the criminal activity, like it was part of their planned programming for the night, and that they would love to see more of it.  It was like "Bob" went around and picked up a bunch of people in his Conversion Van, and said "hey, my name is Bob, I will pay you $300 if you will wear a suit and get on television and state that what the African American's are doing is right.  And, make sure you preach that whites are prejudice against blacks, but that blacks are not prejudice against whites."  The news crews went out early, standing in street corners waiting for violence, like they do before a hurricane hits a beach in North Carolina.   That was the theme and direction of the night, as Bob travelled around in his Conversion Van, picking up as many commentators as he could find, and inciting protestors in Oakland, California and other places that networks were hoping to get burned buildings and high ratings from.   Why should good win, when evil has better ratings?

It was even more evident after all the big four liberal networks (CNN, NBC, CBS, ABC) started announcing businesses were lining up to go back into business in Iran after the Iran deal was signed in July, 2015. Who in their right mind (besides Bob) would send an employee they care about into a country that they arrest and hold individuals who do not think like them, or that are Judeo-Christians? People in Iran are protected by the Iranian government when they perform terrorist activities against the US and Israel, and many are cheered in open squares for performing terroristic acts. How can we imagine sending employees into Iran to work, when they (Iranians) hold American hostages? In fact, like the Iran deal was designed by Bob himself, there was no agreement of releasing a Christian hostage being held in Iran during the Iranian nuclear deal discussions. Saeed Abedini, and Iranian-American, who is a Protestant Christian converted from Shia Muslim, with a wife and 2 children in the US, has been held prisoner in Iran since the summer of 2012. His charges were that he tried to undermine the Iranian government by converting people in Iran to Christianity. None of the four liberal networks said anything, but at least Fox took the other side. How could the four liberal networks state the same retarded thing, except they were trying to sell us (the sheep) like a sly multi-level marketing product, how great the Iranian deal is, in line with Bob's agenda and master plan? In reality, a real story that a news analyst could write about is the fact that the Iranian government already has nuclear bombs, like Pakistan, Israel, Syria, North Korea, and India, and is perfecting the platforms to deliver them with, such as the Fateh-313 or Conqueror missile. No media organization even spoke on this probability, that Iran is already a nuclear threat and its people would likely take any American it could get its hands on as Political prisoners for negotiations. It was like "Bob" was riding around in his Conversion Van again, and went by a few businesses, and said "hey, I will give you $2,000 if you will get on television and tell the people that your company is going to expand and do business in Iran. It doesn't really matter if you never send people into Iran to do business." And then Fox News, in the exact opposite fashion, discussed that the Iranian deal was the worst deal in the history of the world, and that we were all about to get blown up by an Iranian terrorist cell. There is no independent thought coming out of any of the networks, laying out the facts of what the deal was about and why it was good or bad for America; just heads talking that it was a great deal or a bad deal. Then, a news reporter asked the President a hard question about the Iran deal, one that would require an honest answer, and he freaked out, like "how dare you ask me a question like that? Bob would never ask me that question on national television." We, as American's, are losing one of the greatest assets we have ever had, and no one can realize it. We are losing the freedom of the press to investigate, print the truth, and tell the story to inform us. This degradation of the freedom of the press, destroyed by being called "racist" or "anti-women," or "anti-sematic," is in fact anti-truth seeking. News today only seeks stories that it can publish so as not to offend everyone. Truth does not matter anymore. Instead, we are being sold Bob's agenda, and we are saying nothing about it. I never heard what happened to this reporter who asked the President a "truth" based question, but "Bob" probably had him demoted and he may never ask news questions again. No one will tell the Emperor that he is wearing no clothes, because he is a black man and it might offend him, and it will be off script from Bob's Communist agenda. If you ask an African American President a question that he does not like, then you must be a racist. "Everything is ok. Go back to eating your grass and drinking your water." This has truly been the worst eight years this country has ever seen, in that there is no longer any true analysis of what truth is on television, but a dumbing down of information into talking heads, given a news script by Bob, with no analysis. Some of the facts that were obviously overlooked include that "every country that wants a nuclear bomb over the last few years owns one." Duh! The entire conversation between the US and Iran was ludicrous, and designed for us sheep to continue eating our grass while the Emperor takes care of our well-being, and laughingly pisses in our water supply. Iran dreams of the day it can destroy the US and Israel. While Israel is the Holy Land, the US has become the land of "anti-Bible" and "anti-Christian." Israel will be protected by God. The protection of America by God is questionable, although he has his people that he will protect. As asked by Lot, "will you destroy Sodom if there is one good man?"

Bob's agenda has won in every turn over the last eight years. If the people don't support it, then Bob gets on television to justify why the Supreme Court needs to make a decision that "we the people cannot make anymore, because we are not smart enough." We the people are not smart enough to make decisions anymore, except to elect men like Marion Berry to Mayor of Washington, DC after he is convicted of smoking Crack and hiring prostitutes while in office, or supporting Hillary Clinton for President, although she knowingly has lied to "we the people," as her husband did before. She is not even a good liar, although Bob supports her on 4 of the 5 television stations as the greatest candidate eve. , who is one of the most selfish people in the world. It is like we are seeking to instill a monarchy in power. What country would want to do business with a known and open liar, or with someone who always is seen as taking advantage of others in negotiations?  However, Bob likes this decision.  Bob publicizes and portrays whatever the seemingly "Communist" agenda dictates.  Bob lumps us all into groups, and my group, the white, Judeo-Christian male, is losing again, as I can remember the history of Iran holding the hostages in 1979.  We lost against Gay Marriage.  The majority of "we the people" did not want it.  We lost against the Healthcare Fiasco that no one wanted.  We lost against lotteries we did not want, toll roads, lack of funding for our military, welfare reform, the right to say we will not perform Gay Marriages in our churches, the right to teach right and wrong as discussed in the Bible in public schools, and increased scrutiny against Judeo-Christian white males by the IRS.  A bakery owner was even sued and had to pay money because the owner of a private business chose not to do business with a gay couple.  A Court Clerk that issued marriage licenses in Kentucky was put in jail for refusing to give our gay marriage licenses, which cannot even be filled out correctly as it asks who the Groom and Bride are.  Do gay people just choose, "I will pretend I am the man and you pretend you are the woman."  We live in a time of make believe.  Since when can a business not reserve the right to do business with or not do business with anyone they want?  The most neglected individual in the world, the white "heterosexual" male, is now labelled "white privilege," like there is some group trying to look after us white people's future.  He must be hiding in the bushes because I have never found him.  Oh white privilege dude, come out!!  I am a white male and I want some of that white privilege.  Do I need to fill out an application?  And, we are losing in the election scene, as we are asking for people to come to the polls and show that they are American citizens and legally be able to vote, and Bob is stating that requiring a person to prove his identity is racist.

Bob is blasting this on television saying this is racist, so they can keep sending fake voters in masses to polls with no identification, to elect men like Marion Berry. No one will speak up for truth, because people seeking truth are called racist. Identification Cards can be obtained at any Department of Motor Vehicle Office for about $10. Identification Cards are used for welfare, to take a bus trip, to get on an airplane, to get a marriage certificate, and for everything else in the world....but to prove someone is who they say they are to vote is racist. Bob's agenda is the only right agenda. For those who call it into question, we are racist. "That which is wrong will be called right, and that which is right will be called wrong." Well, I am not a racist, but I am tired of the lack of truth. I am tired of the truth being distorted because "Bob" can ride around in a Conversion Van, pick up homeless people, dress them and put them on television, and call them "experts." On CNN you see them all the time, "let's bring in our resident expert, Bob Smith, who is going to tell us why Iran is now our friend. Bob, tell us why Iran is our friend." "Oh yes, Iran is now our friend. They like us and want to do business with us. They have changed a lot since 1979. We know they don't have nuclear weapons and are not trying to obtain them." It is stupid and sickening, and we sheep are tired of hearing it, although we sheep are not speaking up loud enough. We just eat our grass and drink our tainted water. Oh, fracking doesn't hurt anyone. Just ask our neighbors in Texas who have to now drink bottled water. We American humans are retards.

Chapter (5) They Think We Can't Think

*In November 1979, thousands of Iranians stormed the American embassy in Tehran, and held 66 American's hostage for 444 days. However, six consular workers managed to escape, and* hid out in the homes of Canadian diplomats. To get them out of the country unnoticed, the CIA established a fake movie production. As the Iranian's were burning US flags, and screaming anti US everything, the CIA used this fake movie production to get these 6 individuals out of Iran. This rescue effort included putting fake ads in Variety and the Hollywood reporter. This later became a move which came out in 2012 named "Argo." Things in Iran have become sinisterly worse since 1979, creating relationships with proxy parties throughout the world that conduct terrorist acts.

Having "Bob" on television has changed my thoughts on the world. After the rioting in Missouri, I began thinking that all black people must be racist, and that they are formulating a government that is designed against the Judeo-Christian white male, the same men who primarily built this country. But, I don't want to think that way, and know a lot of black people who are not racist. Like Bernice, who gave my daughter a dog. And, all the black people at work. And, all the black people that I have played sports with and been in the military with. So, who are all of these black people who are creating this apparent black racism thing, and why do I feel black people are racist after watching television? Bob just wants me to think that way. I have to watch my mind, as I know the average black male and female do not want to be racist, or appear racist. I know black men and women from work that are not racist, and I apologize to them to lump them in with the extremist African American's who burn down buildings and are against justice and the American way of life. To watch it on television just seems to portray it, to a white male. However, Bob's agenda makes me often question the African American movement in Washington,

DC and their agenda.  I mean, in my mind, how could any black people be agreeing with burning down buildings in Ferguson, and why are no black people  coming on television condemning Mr. Brown for theft and attacking a Police Officer.  Why don't they Police their ranks?  Did Bob overlook trying to find a black person to state destruction of personal and real property is a crime? I remember watching NBC News the next morning after the looting, running down the streets and burning and thinking, "well the President or another African American will be on television this morning condemning this action." Instead, I saw division. White people were on television defending the Police Officer for protecting himself.  African Americans were on television screaming the Police Officer must be charged for killing the stoned, out of compliance, teenager who attacked him.  In my mind, I started thinking of other areas of the world where something like this happened before, where whole groups of people started rallying against other races.  For example, the Extreme Muslims in Iran and Syria, who want to kill all American's and Jews, train for the day they can behead an infidel.  In North Korea, Kim Jong-Un dreams of the day he can blow up America, and has a video displaying such with Michael Jackson's song "We are the World,"  playing in the background.  Also, Nazi Germany, where the German Nazi's initially took guns from Jews, and then marked their businesses so no one would buy from them, then started demanding them leave the country, and then rounded them up and killed them. Evil groups of people do exist around the world, and they do operate in bands of people, like apes do in the jungle, doing what the strongest ape tells them.

As I watched re-runs of the men running down the street on television after the no indictment against the Police Officer was given, I started feeling more and more insecure in my own country. Are the black people in high places in government trying to take over the country like in Nazi Germany? Did no African American's think the looting and burning of buildings was wrong? Are black people in positions of government throughout the US controlling what is being placed on television? Why are not more African American people speaking out about the entire burning down of a town? Where were the black people I had worked with that I thought were my friends, and that were just American Judeo-Christians like me, except in black skin? Were they only pretending to like me and to follow the laws of the Bible and really hated me and wanted to kill and enslave white people? Why did the President of the United States, an African American who was supposed to stand for law and order and the Constitution and unity, not step out and try to bring white people and black people back together? Why is no one else questioning how the Chicago political machine controlled the elections in 2008 and 2012 by massing the black vote in polls with fake names, and how large African American "Associations" were sending huge amounts of African American's around America to protest, while being paid for such by a billionaires from Hungary? Why do journalists question the ability of men and women to get an identification card to vote with, when there is no question that they need identification to get Social Security Disability, welfare, get on an airplane, or to register for a class at a college? At this point, I had to turn off the television. "Bob" had conveniently made me paranoid about a lot of issues. In fact, Bob made me start question myself if I am now or ever have been racist?

Chapter (6) Racism

*"On September 11, 2001, two planes were flown into the World Trade Center by Jihad terrorists, and one into the Pentagon. A*

*fourth plane was taken over by terrorists, but the passengers*
*took it upon themselves to take back over the plane or die*
*trying. The plane was flying a routine flight from Newark, New*
*Jersey to San Francisco, California. While it is not known what*
*the intended target of the plane was, it was believed that the*
*plane was to hit the White House or The Capitol Building. The*
*passengers will forever be known as hero's for standing up and*
*fighting back against the evil plans that was unfolding that day.*
*A memorial is set up for them at the crash site in Stoney creek*
*Township, Pennsylvania, and is called the Flight 93 National*
*Memorial. "*

Growing up in Charlotte, North Carolina, I never thought I
was around racism. In the area that I grew up in, there were
not a lot of black people, but there were in other sections of
Charlotte. One young African American male I grew up with
was one of the greatest pitchers I ever saw in Little League. I
remember being on a baseball team with him at Mint Hill,
looking at this African American kid and thinking how I wanted
to be able to pitch like him. I was always lucky to get walked by
him, because he usually struck me out. He had good parents
and his father worked in construction, which a lot of our fathers
did in that time. He was invited to everything, and I never
thought of racism against him. In fact, I wanted to be him.
Another young African American male I grew up with was a
great artist. I remember wanting to draw as good as he could. I
was actually jealous of some of his art work. I was jealous of
many blacks when I played basketball, football, and in the
classroom. To me growing up in the seventies and eighties,
they were just black kids, but they were competitive like I was.
If I described a white kid who lived down the road, I would just
say kid. If it was a black, Hispanic, Chinese, or Indian kid, I
would usually add the adjective in front of the name, like

Chinese kid.  When I ran cross country, I ran with one of the fastest runners in Charlotte who was an African American.  He ran early in the morning, even on days when we had cross country practice to increase his times.  I still run early in the mornings today probably because I still want to be fast like him.  The greatest African American kid I ever saw was Michael Jordan.  We all wanted to be like Michael Jordan, and he was the face of the all American African American.  There was no racism on either side that I knew of surrounding Michael Jordan.

However, I remember that since there were not a lot of African American kids near where I grew up, that they would bus additional African American's to my side of town.  These kids would get up and get on a bus around 6am every morning in West Charlotte to make it to Mint Hill by 7:30am.  At the time it did not make any sense to me or my parents, but what Charlotte was trying to do was diversify.  At the schools I attended in Charlotte, I never felt racism against anyone. I can remember one white guy who had a blue Chevrolet truck who would drive into the parking lot of Independence High School every day waving two big Confederate Flags in the back.  I never felt like it was flown to show racism, but just showing his personality. He chewed tobacco and played Hank Williams, Jr. real loud, and had beer drinking parties that I, the nerdish kid was never invited to, and this was seen as his personality. Looking back, I guess some of the African American kids in the school probably thought he was racist too, to fly those flags in his truck, like a Jewish person would take offense to a person who had a tattoo of a Swastika on his arm.  However, I do not think anything was ever said. When I got old enough to date, I never wanted to date an African American, but I don't think they ever were interested in me either.  White people typically dated white people, and black people typically dated black people.  At my high school prom, I cannot remember any mixed couples, although there may have been and I just cannot remember.  As I have gotten older, I have noticed this trend among most races; Indians typically marry other Indians, blacks typically marry other blacks, whites typically marry other whites, Asians typically marry other Asians; Mexican's usually marry other Mexican's.  There is a small percentage that marry occasionally inter-racially, such as white and South Korean, but for the most part races marry, go to church, and are buried in segregated cemeteries.  I don't think its racist; I just think we are attracted and belong in our types, like animals are attracted to their types. However, one of the most important verses of the Bible is when Miriam was upset with Moses for marrying an Ethiopian woman, and God gave Miriam leprosy for her being upset with him.  God does not apparently see anything wrong with whites or olive skinned people marrying blacks or any other race.  Paul says it best when he said he wishes we would just remain celibate and not wed, like he and Jesus did.

However, God did separate the races.  Babylon was a city, whose ruins lay in modern day Iraq.  It was built by the Amorites in or around 1800 Before Christ (BC).  It was located in a fertile plain between the Tigris and Euphrates Rivers.  Babylon was ruled by the famous leader Hammurabi, who created many of the judicial laws still used in the US today.  The hanging gardens in Babylon became one of the seven-wonders of the world.  It was estimated that Babylon was the largest city in the world for about 100 years (1770 BC to 1670 BC).  Babylon is first mentioned in the Bible in Genesis 11, when the people attempted to build a tower that would reach to heaven, and the Lord said, "If as one people speaking the same language they have begun to do this, then nothing they plan to do will be impossible for them.  Come, let us go down and confuse their language so they will not understand each other." From there, it is believed that the races were separated to different ends of the earth, and that peoples spoke different languages. Following this, Isaiah, a prophet in the Bible, began to prophesy around 740 BC, and one of his predictions was about the fall of Babylon. "Behold, I will stir up the Medes against them, who will not regard silver; and as for gold, they will not delight in it. Also their bows will dash the young men to pieces, and they will have no pity on the fruit of the womb; their eye will not spare children. And Babylon, the glory of the kingdoms, the beauty of the Chaldean's pride, will be as when God overthrew Sodom and Gomorrah. It will never be inhabited, nor will it be settled from generation to generation; nor will the Arabian pitch tents there, nor will the shepherds make their sheepfolds there." (Isaiah 13:17-20) When Isaiah made this prediction, the Medes (Iranians) were too weak, and were ruled by other nations. Nebuchadnezzar became king of Babylon around 605 BC. At this time, Babylon was the leading empire in the world, with beautiful palaces, city streets, and temples. By the time Nebuchadnezzar died (after he went crazy and ate grass), the city was a fortress. It had two very thick walls, and a large moat. However, on a day around 539 BC, when the Babylonians were celebrating a feast, the Medes and Persians entered and took over Babylon without a battle. Today, Babylon is still an empty city, as forecast by Isaiah 200 years before the Mede and Persian invasion. Saddam Hussein dreamed of rebuilding the city and its glory.

## Chapter (7)   Separate but not Equal

*When I got out of high school and joined the Marines, some of the first words I heard drill instructors say were "you are not*

*white, black, Latino, Chinese, or anything else in the Marine*
*Corps. You are dark green or light green. Do you understand?"*


    I went to an African American church once in Vienna, Virginia and none of the black people in the church spoke to me. They all smiled at me, but they gave me a look like I was there to spy on them, and not to get closer to God and his word. In truth, I am always trying to get closer to the understanding of God and his will (and even his person), and was trying to that night, thinking I was going into a white Baptist Church, but was wrong. Then, after I was inside, sitting on a pew, being embarrassed to be the only white person in the church, I was afraid to leave lest people thought I had no respect for God's house. It was a good message, but I felt out of place. Likewise, I am sure that there are black people who have been to white churches in America, and they were not spoken to and felt out of place. We are as human beings, divided by race because it is obvious. Our skin color is different. To notice this difference in skin color for a white person today is racist. For a black person to call a white person a "white person" or even "cracker" is normal. However, the Bible says not to judge if a man marries another race, as Moses married an Ethiopian woman, and God gave Miriam leprosy for saying something to Moses about it. And, the Bible says we will all be in heaven, if we accept Jesus Christ as our Lord and Savior, whether we are black, white, blue, or green. The key thing on marriage given is that you are not to be unevenly yoked; such as if you are a hard-working, Judeo-Christian woman and you are married to a fence sitting, lazy, unemployed man whose hobbies include drinking beer. I do not believe race has anything to do with being unevenly yoked, but laziness and moral values does. In dealing with Oxen, to be unevenly yoked means one Ox is pulling more weight than the other Ox.

When I got out of high school and joined the Marines, some of the first words I heard drill instructors say were "you are not white, black, Latino, Chinese, or anything else in the Marine Corps. You are dark green or light green. Do you understand?" The Marine Corps would not tolerate racism, and every race has had hero's throughout all of the American wars, including in the War of 1812, where General "Stonewall" Jackson put together the first hodgepodge of soldiers, including a white militia from Tennessee, black "free men," French pirates, and members of the US Army, Navy and Marines. These separate but equal races kicked butt in the War of 1812, and killed over 2000 British soldiers whereas only 13 of the hodgepodge American "soldiers" were killed. From the very beginning, America has been a melting pot of different races, and has been seemingly blessed because of such. In fact, it is the largest amount of races since God separated the races at Babylon. Do you think the re-assembly of the races in America is in line with God's will? I have often wondered that, as we can now with modern technology speak each other's language for the first time since he separated us.

Recently, I was speaking to a black man who served in the US Army and was from Chicago, Illinois. He told me the story about his family being brought up in a poor part of Chicago, and that he went in certain areas of Chicago, but was told as a black man that he was not allowed to go in certain other areas because he was black and not white, and that they would not put up with black people in these areas. Now, this sounded like racism. I never saw or heard this anywhere in North Carolina, but it sounded like I would finally hear about what the racism thing really was about in modern society.  Anyway, he said that his two brothers were in jail for dealing drugs, and that he was the only one in his family that got out.  He said he was embarrassed to go back to Chicago because he lived in a nice neighborhood in Kansas now and drove a nice car, and did not take his family back there (to Chicago) because it would embarrass him.  So, in my mind I started thinking there must be racism in the world, and especially in Chicago, that I do not fully understand about. The problem is I am a non-racist white male who now realizes that he is looked down on by others because he is white.  Some people out of Chicago must think, "hey that is a white guy.  He must be racist."  The truth is, I am a white guy , with a family, that wants to be left alone and not to be scared for my children going down the roads at any time because someone (of any race) might rob them or hurt them.  And, many blacks judge me because my ancestors were white, not understanding that my ancestors were slaves once also.  If you are a hard working black man or woman, or of any other race, I want you to make money, be able to take care of your family, and enjoy the piece of the pie that is provided by this great country of America.  If you own a restaurant, I will buy food from you, and if you own a bank I will put my money in your bank.  However, I too want this opportunity, and I do not want to be judged and put down because I am white.  And, if I accidentally say "that is a black man," I want the words to be taken in the context that you are a black man, and that I don't look down on you for that.  It is just a fact.  You have black skin, whether you can accept it or not.  I want safety, peace, economic security, honesty, and to know I can get old and not be left somewhere penniless to die.  This is the America that my ancestor's built over the last two hundred years for all of us; white, black, Chinese, Japanese, Indian's. Social Security and other benefits help take care of us when we cannot take care of ourselves, as well as welfare, WIK, and other government subsidies I contribute to as I work.  And, I don't mind contributing to these things as I know I may one day need any of these.  As a white male living today, I cannot help that your African American ancestors were placed in slavery in the 1800's, much like you cannot help my ancestors were once slaves and indentured servants from England and other European countries.  Also, you cannot help that the Jewish people have been enslaved, tortured, impaled, hung on a cross, and burned throughout history.  African American people cannot help the plight of the Jewish people, including when they were enslaved in Egypt, an African country.  Should modern day African's be held accountable for their having kept Israeli's as slaves 4000 years ago?

George Santayana was first coined as saying "those who fail to learn from the mistakes of their predecessors are destined to repeat them."  This was so evident from the beginning of America.  Christopher Columbus, who in the late 1400's thought he had found a Westerly route to Asia, instead found the Arawak men and women on the coast of South America. Columbus could not find gold on the island, so he took the people as slaves, and delivered them back to Europe, beginning a slave trade.  The Arawak men and women were so free with their possessions that they shared with everyone, and did not fight back well.  Between the years 1495 and 1650, it is estimated that Spaniards had killed over 300,000 Arawak men and women, who were living freely on the islands.  These people did not even wear clothes, like Adam and Eve before they knew the difference between being clothed.  We had the slavery of the Indian's, which killed a bunch of non-violent people, and then we went right into slavery of African American's and European's, under the same premise.  Very wealthy men, with their eyes on more wealth and power, enslave peoples for their own purposes. This is truth. This is still happening today with slavery for prostitution, labor, and the porn industry. The problem today is that most American's cannot see that this could happen to them. They cannot see that they have given up their First Amendment Rights (Freedom of Speech), and that the next election will be toward giving up gun rights (Second Amendment of freedom to bear arms). After that, slavery will become inevitable for the working class man under the wealthy. This is completely against what our forefathers wanted. We judge North Korea as bad, and want freedom for their people, too blind to see our future generations will be as bad off as they are. Freedom of the Press is down. Gun Rights is next. Enslavement and big brother's manifestations, like Kim Jong-un are next.

There are happenings throughout America right now that are not right. There are attacks on the America that I love that are taking away from my security blanket that I can get old and enjoy living in the land of the free. I am becoming increasingly concerned that groups of unknown people are trying to start a race war, and are going to try to repeat the history of Nazi Germany by trying to eradicate white people. These groups are being led by "Bob," the talking heads on at least four out of the five large networks. And Bob, gets African American's on television to start an agenda, and dares anyone to disagree with them or he will call them a racist. For example, an African American State Senator in South Carolina introducing new restrictions on buying guns. If you disagree with him, then you are a racist and support Dylann Roof's killing of 9 black people in a Charleston church. Never mind that an 11 year old girl was able to keep herself from being raped by shooting a home invader. We twist truths to fit our agenda. Answer this oh intelligent, law abiding State Senator, "what laws are you enacting to get hand guns and rifles out of the hands of criminals and the mentally ill?" He would respond, that is a racist statement, as many criminals are African American's. We are now hidden from the truth under the word "racism." It is no longer separate but equal, as there is no even feigned equality here. The word "racist" is being used against white people like the word "Jew" was being used against Jewish people before they were exterminated like bugs in World War II.

I am very concerned that the large majority of African American people, who are like I am and just want to be able to work hard and have a life and have our laws and freedoms left alone, are not going to be strong enough to stand up to these African American leaders who want to take over the country, just like the average German who disagreed with the policies of Nazi Germany could not stand up against Nazi policies. The attacks against the ethnic groups have begun: and I am afraid it could turn into something like Nazi Germany, especially how we keep overlooking parts of our history. We keep hiding flags, protesting building names and statues, changing our history books, re-writing history, refocusing away from the bad stuff so we can only look at the good. God works through both the good and evil. When we forget the evil, we are apt to do it all over again. For example, no one ever teaches in our American history how the Indian's, who were living pretty blessed and happy lives in America, were tortured, killed, enslaved, displaced, seduced by alcohol, and moved from place to place like gypsies, and finally exterminated like bugs to make way for the "manifest destiny" of the new European settlers. We overlook parts of history, and by doing such, we are apt to repeat the same retarded mistakes. This enslavement thing has repeated itself time and time again through history, and as we hide history, it is going to happen again, just like it is happening today in North Korea, several African nations, and throughout South America. "Bob," pays no attention to the plight of the people in North Korea, Africa, or South America, because he secretly supports it.   We don't pay attention to slavery today, because it is not the black man or woman in chains like we envision from the 1800s, and is instead children in labor camps that are being forced to marry young, older people being placed in slavery because they cannot pay their nursing home costs, and the government and other agencies taking everything people worked for.  Young women and men around the world are being placed in slavery as prostitutes.  Many people place themselves in slavery through their own sins and addictions, such as through alcohol, sex, and drugs.  They become enslaved to feed their addictions, which Bob gladly provides for them. And the war on the drug dealers in South America, is a joke.  We pretend to try to stop the flow of drugs coming into North America, while at the same time legalizing the same drugs for sale in Colorado.  Marijuana harms young people's brain cells, makes them lazy and lethargic.  If you wanted to enslave an entire generation of young people, the smartest way to do so is to let them all get high, as they are all lethargic and apathetic, with no creative thoughts left.

## Chapter (8) Overlooked History

"A man gets drunk.  He wakes up late the next morning for work.  He promises never to drink again.  On Saturday night he has a bottle of alcohol in front of him again."

"The reason the Roman Empire and the British Empire's both fell was because they got fat, lazy, stupid, and were intoxicated and *could not see it coming. America is following in the same footsteps."*

*Napoleon tried to invade Russia, then Hitler tried the same tactic, both having tremendous casualties.*

Before we get started, let's look at some recent history:

- At 12:10 am on June 13, 1994 Nicole Brown Simpson and Ronald Goldman were found murdered outside a Brentwood area of Los Angeles. Evidence found and collected at the scene indicated that OJ Simpson was the murderer. The world watched as the Police tried to stop him in his White Ford Bronco, as he led Police on a chase throughout Los Angeles and back to his home. After the most watched trial in history, OJ was acquitted for the murders, mainly through botched Police work. African American's everywhere celebrated. There were no riots in the streets or looted Wal-Mart stores for the dead bodies of Nicole Simpson or Ronald Goldman. Nicole Simpson and Ronald Goldman's killer got off, although he was arrested for other felonies and went bankrupt in the future. Their bodies continue to rot in the grave, wanting justice but likely to see none in this lifetime. It is my opinion, OJ beat this trial, but God is waiting for him on the other side. This trial is rarely discussed any more, as history has forgotten.
- On February 26, 2012 George Zimmerman, a Hispanic Male, shot and killed an African American male, in an altercation at a housing community. George Zimmerman was always called a white male by the press, and this became a white on black crime, instead

of a Hispanic on black crime.  "Bob" played this trial for all it was worth, trying to feed the masses that white people were racist against black people.  George Zimmerman, the Hispanic male, was acquitted on 2nd Degree murder charges on July 16, 2013.  When he was acquitted, African American's looted a Wal-Mart store in Los Angeles, and a separate one near Jacksonville, Florida and "Bob" never said this was wrong.  It is still to this day called a white on black crime, in an attempt to keep Hispanics from being a separate racial group so that they don't have discriminatory rights.  The truth is most Hispanic's work circles around other races, especially in construction, agriculture, and domestic type jobs.  It is unknown what would happen to the American economy if Hispanics went back home, and whites and blacks were required to perform manual labor again.

- On October 6, 2012 a white, unarmed 18 year old male under the influence of drugs was shot and killed by a black Police Officer in Mobile, Alabama.  Although there was public pressure to bring an indictment by a Grand Jury against the Police Officer, none was ever brought and the case made little news outside of Mobile.  The discrepancy of the press coverage was not mentioned in the local press, but was tweeted and made national headlines across Facebook and other Social media outlets, which appear to show more honest and true coverage of events than even the major networks can provide.  The black Police Officer probably should have been indicted, but white people did not burn down Papa John's Pizza's or loot Wal-Mart.

- On August 11, 2014, in Salt Lake City, Utah, Police responded to reports of a man waving a gun outside of a 7-11. When Police arrived, they noticed a group of 3 boys matching the description of the call. A white subject, wearing headphones, reached down to pull up his pants and a black Police Officer shot him. The black Police Officer was never charged with a crime regarding this, although the suspect's family requested an investigation. This shooting barely made the news, and when reported the description of the Police Officer was only that he was "non-white." There was no looting at Wal-Mart, no burning down of buildings or busing rioters in from Chicago to protest this young white man's shooting from a black Police Officer. This barely made the news, and the kid will never breathe air on this side of life again.

- On December 12, 2014 David Ruenzel was shot and killed while hiking at a park in Oakland, California. Police are seeking two black males as suspects. Ruenzel was a professional "anti-racial" author who wrote articles for the Southern Poverty Law Center supporting oppressed African American males. The same type people he wrote about and tried to protect; killed him. This is in line with Madilyn Murray O'Hair, the leader of the American atheist movement, who was kidnapped, murdered, and mutilated along with her son, John Garth Murray and granddaughter Robin Murray O'Hair by a fellow member of her American Atheist group, so he could steal her money. There was no respect for Mr. Ruenzel and his work, even after his death. Mr. Ruenzel had spent the last few years of his life writing about "white privilege" when he was killed by the 2 black males. Even after his killing by 2 black males, NPR radio had a guest on the show that spoke on how his death was "created" by his own white privilege, instead of that 2 black men broke one of God's oldest Commandment's, "thou shalt not kill." It was not the black person's indifference of right and wrong, but Mr. Ruenzel's being born a white male who made him be killed by 2 black males, and this was preached on National Public Radio to the masses like we (the sheep) are all supposed to believe this. Bob owns the message line on National Public Radio, and preaches messages like this to the masses no matter what we really believe because he wants to change our thought processes, like accepting Transvestite Males being able to use the women's restrooms.

- On March 30, 2015 a 50 year old white male was travelling on a Philadelphia, Pennsylvania rail train and was severely beaten by approximately 12 African American males on the train. This was recorded on video, and the Police stated they were going to release the video but never did. As of this date, no arrests have been made for this beating although a picture of all of these African American males was captured on a non-disclosed video. The Police Chief initially stated he would release the video to try to find the suspects, and then he never released the video. He knew people would know who these thugs were, but he did not want to catch them. Bob never discussed this on the large networks, and this man's beating still has no justice.
- On March 30, 2015 David Autry was travelling on a St Louis Metro link train, and was severely beaten by three African American males because he did not want to talk

about the Michael Brown incident. They beat him; it was on video, yet the news media (Bob) did not record it or want it to go public because it would cause a stir that African American males beat a white male. Mr. Autry posted on a u-tube video the actual attack and the disturbance of African American on White violence that is now occurring. It has made very little media attention, however.

- On July 4, 2015 a white man was severely beaten by six black males in Cincinnati, Ohio after a hip hop concert. The beating of the white man by the six black males is on camera, and clearly shows the man being beaten. A Cincinnati Police Officer originally labelled the crime as a hate crime, but then the Police Chief, probably following a phone call from Washington, DC relayed to the press that the release of the crime as a "hate crime" was possibly a mistake. Bob quickly followed suit, and all the talking heads started saying this was not a hate crime, although to us white people it was clearly a hate crime being covered up. If it was six white males beating one black male after a Hank Williams Jr. concert would it be a mistake to label it a hate crime? The sheep said nothing about this, and continued grazing.

- On July 5, 2015 a white woman was shot in the back of the head in Hollywood, California with a shotgun by a black male, with no apparent motive while she walked with her white boyfriend on the beach. The suspect was black male wearing dark clothing and a hoodie. It is not known why the white male was not shot. This has not been labelled a hate crime at this time, and Bob thought this too unimportant to report on.

- On August 27, 2015 a television reporter and cameraman were shot during a live broadcast by a bitter, ex-television reporter. Vester Lee Flanagan shot up to 24 times at point black range at 24 year old Reporter Alison Parker and cameraman Adam Ward, who were both white. Vester Flanagan was black, and said he shot them because he was upset over the shootings in Charleston, SC, because Alison Parker had gone to Human Resources against him, and because he was let go from his job.

While these are just a few examples of black on white crimes, they are being given to show that black on white crimes are actually as prevalent as white on black crimes, but that the media would for some reason have us believe otherwise, even on the case above. The black guy who shot two media workers on live television made less news, and there are no protests that the Michael Brown shooting by a Police Officer after Michael Brown tried to take his gun. It is like the media is trying to make white people look virulently racist, when most white people I have ever met are like me, and don't even discuss race. It's like homosexuality. I never vehemently became against homosexuality until I had to watch Bob on television telling me on the 6'o clock news that homosexuality is great, and that people against it are homophobic, like I have a problem. Homosexuality is against my Bible, the same book that formed the foundation of most of the laws and government of America. However, my Bible tells me not to sit in judgement of another man who is sinning. So, I just don't want to know about it, just like it used to be in the military. "Don't ask, Don't tell," was a great policy in the military. No one wanted to know about it. Today, there are Lesbian, Bi-Sexual, Gay, Transgender (LBGT) Barbecues in the military, and if you don't show up and support the cause you are against it.  The truth is I don't care what another man or woman does in their private lives, and behind closed doors they are now protected by the 4th Amendment as long as they don't hurt anyone else.  However, don't make me think it is alright because I should not have to change my beliefs because a man chooses to have sex with another man instead of with a woman.  It is sick to me, and I don't want to think about it, as I believe in God and his words.

Chapter (9) You Have to Laugh

*On August 11, 2015 a British Special Air Service (SAS) Sniper saved a father and his eight year old son from being beheaded by an Islamic State of Iraq and Syria (ISIS) maniac in Syria.  The special forces sniper killed the murderer, and then killed two other members of the terror group helping with the execution.  The ISIS militants had labelled them "infidels" and stated they must die because they refused to denounce their faith.*

It is sometimes funny, as it is white people on television talking about how racist white America is.  Do not any of them, as they read the tele-prompters to the masses of sheep, question what they are reading, or are their salaries so high that they just say whatever is put in front of them, like a Chinese or North Korean journalist?  To me race is never an issue, or it wasn't until every television station in America started making it an issue, and the President and his wife started making it their Political trump card.  "Oh, you are against Obama Care, you must be racist.  Oh, you are against my Iran deal that never went before Congress. You must be racist. etc."   However, the question then becomes, why?  What are we dealing with here?  Why does the press want to have the untrue vision that more black people are hurt by white people that white people by black people?  Why would so many people celebrate OJ Simpson getting off for murder, instead of seeking justice for the victim's?  Why is the press so quiet about the increased number of attacks on Police Officers?  And then, it came to me. We are not dealing with an attack by human beings and their intelligence and powers.  We are being attacked by Satan and his demonic forces.  Satan has lead government leaders throughout history.  As Jesus was going through his 40 day fast, Satan approached him and showed him all the kingdoms of the world and how he would give them all to him if he would bow down to him.  Demonic forces have become in control of the owners of the newspapers, media, and other organizations, thus leading to this dumbing down of America.  Today, better news (truth) is given through social media and twitter than by CNN, NBC, CBS, and ABC, as it is usually not filtered out to make the correct agenda statement.  However, technology has been taken over by Satan, and it is with a high probability that Bob can even filter what is placed on twitter and social media through the use of his thugs.  And, we human beings, without the capacity to understand, are becoming like apes;  only doing what the lead ape is doing, unable to think for ourselves or give our own opinion for being considered an outsider of the group. As much as hundreds of thousands of us have worked to become Judeo-Christians and to become closer to God and to follow his tenants, thousands of others have now given their souls to Satan, including many media moguls,  thus leading to reporting that is spoken of in the Bible.  In 2 Timothy 3 it states, "in the last days, perilous times shall come.  For men shall be lovers of their own selves, covetous, boasters, proud, blasphemers, disobedient to parents, unthankful, unholy. Without natural affection, trucebreakers, false accusers, incontinent, fierce, despisers of those that are good, traitors, heady, high minded, lovers of pleasures more than lovers of God; having a form of Godliness, but denying the power thereof; from such turn away." We humans are becoming just like apes, seeking our leader and following whoever speaks the loudest because we are too weak to speak up for ourselves, just like German citizens were when Adolph Hitler became the leader of Germany, with a lot of young men with guns enforcing his laws. What is right has become wrong, and what is wrong has become right. We, as a country are evolving into a country that will by the last days be considered worse than Nazi Germany. God destroyed Babylon through the Medes (Iranians). Are we stupid enough to hide that portion of history, as it is apt to repeat itself? That by which is evil will be considered good, and that which is good will be considered evil. We are in the last days, and we will evolve into apes as we go forward. Charles Darwin was close, when he stated that man evolved from apes. However, in reality his theory was backward in that instead, men are evolving into apes. And Bob, who I thought was the large owners of the media organizations, is in reality Satan himself, leading us within his will toward the final onslaught before the Anti-Christ returns.

### Chapter (10) Apes are Gay

*One day in Montana, 23 year old Raphael Resinde and 26 year old Enrico Garza tried to break into a Montana home. It is unknown if they knew that an 11 year old girl was home; but when they broke in, the girl grabbed her father's 12 gauge Mossberg Shotgun. She shot the first home invader in the abdomen and groin, and the other in the shoulder. Resinde was found to be armed with a 45 caliber handgun that he had stolen from a previous home invasion.*

"The gay relationships that are often shared between men and women are often just like apes. An ape (male or female) often socializes, and defuse tense situations by having sex with other apes. They also show affection to and greet each other through sexual stimulation. While they still have male and female sex with each other for reproduction, it is usually not with long term partners." Therefore, an ape has no moral code such as the Bible gives that Eve was created for Adam, or that sex is to be enjoyed by married couples in the privacy of their own bedrooms. And, Bob wants us to believe that this is natural. The show, "Modern Family" shows two seemingly normal men in a relationship with a daughter and their family and we learn to relate to them, and even like them. Although I am against the sin of homosexuality, I for some reason like the show. Just like a rock is slowly smoothed by passing water, we (including myself) are becoming indifferent to many of the laws that God set in motion. Although God would love both of the men in "Modern Family," he would not appreciate the abomination of the sin that it proudly displays as "ok," and actually destroyed Sodom and Gomorrah for this same activity. Bob wants you to believe that there is no God, and that we were all created by an explosion in outer space. Bob, by the time you die, will create another scientific explanation for man that is beyond Israel's Judeo-Christian explanation of the evolution of humanity. Bob will put it in front of you on television, and make you believe that if you don't believe that it is right, that you are stupid, ignorant, and out of touch with modern civilization; as he did when he supported the Supreme Court making Gay marriage acceptable throughout the blessed nation of America against the wishes of the large proportion of

American's.  The Monarchy that George Washington was so concerned about has arrived.  Put on your wigs!

On July 4, 2015, Independence Day, the first thing I saw on my Facebook Posts was an article from "The State," a newspaper based out of Columbia, SC stating that Episcopalian Pastors are allowing their ministers to be Gay, and the article was written in a fashion that this was the right thing, and that to think otherwise would be wrong.  I do not know what Bible they (the pretend ministers) are using, but mine pretty emphatically spells out that God gave Eve to Adam when he was lonely from a bone in his body, and that a marriage is to be between a man and woman.  Furthermore, the Bible pretty clearly discusses the destruction of Sodom and Gomorrah from where men wanted to have sex with other men, instead of with a woman.  Their need to fulfill their most primal lusts with adultery instead of controlling their sexual desires as the Bible discusses leads to the conclusion of God destroying the city, as well as Lot's wife, who was told not to look back.  This is in tune with how most Junior High Schools in America teach sex education:  no longer is abstinence the preferred method, but birth control (condoms) and the morning after pill.  The difference between men and animals is that men are supposed to be able to control their primal desires, such as sex and anger.  Man can blush, is given rules and laws, and knows right from wrong.  When man gets away from God, he or she becomes out of the will of God.  Man has a soul, and this soul lives on after the body is gone.  God has been very generous and forgiving to America, and has looked over its multitude of sins, I believe, because there are still good men and women in the country, although Bob on CNN, NBC, CBS, and ABC would rather you believe in evolution.  Remember when God was asked if he would destroy the city (Sodom) if there were ten good men, and even one good man?  And then, when the Angel goes to see Lot the men want to have sex with the male Angel instead of having sex with Lot's daughter and a concubine. When we run out of Judeo-Christians in the nation, and we all become like apes, it is with a high probability that God will destroy the America as we know it today. It happened to the Roman Empire. It happened to the British Empire. And, it will happen to America. Judeo-Christians are under attack, not only by Bob, but from our own government. A Fire Chief in February 2015 was fired in Atlanta, Georgia for speaking out against homosexuality. A bakery owner in Portland, Oregon was fined and ordered to pay $135,000 to a gay couple that she refused to bake a cake for their wedding. A precinct in Mississippi was fined $7500 for having prayer in a public school. Court clerks who do not want to perform Gay marriages are being forced to or lose their jobs. One court clerk in Kentucky was put in jail. People in the military are under attack for speaking up against evil in high places. We Judeo-Christians are and will continue to be under attack from evil people until the end of time. However, until then, we Judeo-Christians need to form a plan, and prepare ourselves and our families for our current lives, and the future. The evil that is transcribing this neighbor is also routed in this Gay movement that is taking over America. If a man is Gay, he no longer follows the laws of God in the Bible. One compromise of a moral code makes it easier for the next compromise, and so on. Therefore, he or she no longer feels the need to follow the other laws, such as though should not kill, steal, or bear false witness. In fact, it is with a high probability that a gay man could place his hand on a Bible, affirm he will tell the truth "so help him God" to a judge, and then get on a witness stand and lie about a court case, as he is already ignoring other tenants of God. Our nation was built by men and women who sought to live good lives as taught by the

Bible. They helped to build schools, such as Harvard University, Mercer University, and Wake Forest University that were destined to train Preachers to go out into the flock and teach the word of God. However, Bob influenced man, and then man fell.

It is my opinion that Bob (Satan) will use both the Homosexual movement and the anti-white movement to attack and kill Judeo-Christians throughout America. The time is coming, and the average man will not have the intestinal fortitude to stand up to the virulently evil leaders, just like in Rome where the citizens flocked to attend Gladiator matches to watch men kill each other. The British Empire used to be called the "Empire where the sun never sets." They held colonies on every Continent in the world. Their pride began to wane in 1781, when General Cornwallis was forced to surrender to General George Washington. Everything went downhill from there, and by the end of World War II, it had given freedom to most of the Colonies that it had held. America is next to see the loss of its power, due to the same reasons; pride, lust, laziness, trade imbalances, a feeling of superiority to others, lack of trust in what made America great: God.

When a man disagrees with what Bob is supporting, he will have the full support and weight of the US Government behind him, as the top government leaders must be aligned with Bob. No more attendance to freedom of the press, 1st, 2nd, and 4th Amendments, and the freedom to pursue life, liberty and the pursuit of happiness. Soon, you will have to add "In Bob we trust." The slippery slope leads us to the reduction for the caring of life, just like apes. The compromise of our moral values will destroy the US, and will have a significant impact on the world, as in the past the US has been the Police Officer of the world, and a country that was a beacon of light for peoples who were held in bondage or slavery. We, since 2008, have announced we will no longer be the Police Officer of the world. Luckily, China is stepping up, but to what cost to our own country? In the US, man is now determining that assisted suicide is the right thing, and this will soon go in front of the Supreme Court; who now makes decisions such as this, as the sheep in the Senate and Congress cannot be trusted to make the "right decision." This type of behavior was prevalent on earth before Adam and Eve. Prior to Adam and Eve, a type of human existed on the earth that was animal in nature, with a brain and knowledge, just like apes. They learned how to form weapons, axes, and other tools from metals found in the earth, and lived around the world. However, these humans never had the soul given by God. Adam and Eve were the first human beings that were given a soul, from the breath of God. One of the first instructions given Adam and Eve were not to eat from the tree of the knowledge of Good and Evil, however they ignored that command (at Satan's urging) and we have been under the judgement of almighty God ever since.

### Apes form Groups, and Attack Those They Don't Like

*On or about March 11, 2015, a 19 year old girl, unconscious on a beach chair, was raped on a beach in Panama Beach, Florida with hundreds of people watching and drinking beer, and no one called Police, and no one stepped in to help. The rape was recorded on a mobile phone, which was confiscated during an unrelated investigation regarding a shooting in Troy, Alabama, and more people seemed concerned about spilling their beer than the girl being raped. At least two black men raped her, and they were described as "like wild animals preying on a carcass lying in the woods."*

It is a known fact that Apes form groups and violently kill individuals in neighboring groups in order to expand their own territory. During research conducted by the University of Michigan over a 10 year study, researcher's saw at least 18 fatal attacks (Chimps on chimps), and found evidence of about three others perpetrated by members of a large community of about 150 chimps at Ngogo, Kibale National Park in Uganda. Chimpanzees are known to attack others of their own when they are trying to expand their territory. The Chimpanzees are usually led by one of their own that is the strongest and the most outspoken or loudest. The Chimpanzees, when expanding their territory, will even attack females who are carrying infants. In most of the attacks like this, the infants were killed because they were easy prey. Some of the females that were attacked succumbed to the attack, gave in, and joined the group. This sounds just like gang initiations that are occurring daily throughout America. Girls are "raped" in to the group. Boys go out and kill someone or commit a robbery to be brought in. What is right is wrong, and what is wrong is right.

In Nazi Germany, the Nazi's violently killed individuals in neighboring countries in order to expand their territory. It took nineteen months from the date that Hitler first took power to the date that he began expanding his territory. During these months, Hitler used some sort of "mafia don" mentality to expand his territory. However, Hitler did not want any type of truce or civilized agreement. He did not value life, and believed war to be the only goal of his country, as it was the most profitable economically. Much of the world watched (it won't happen to me) as Hitler spread his empire, and it was only when America was personally attacked at Pearl Harbor by the

Japanese, that we (the US) became involved in stopping the evil that was spread by the threats and loud mouth of Hitler. The group had been formed. For Germans, they had to join with the Nazi regime or fear being killed, not only men but women and children also, just like the Chimpanzee's described previously. If they did not join the group, they might have their property taken away and themselves imprisoned at one of the concentration camps as attackers. They had to be against the Jews, the blessed people who had actually loaned money to the Germans and other European countries to help spread economic progress, and build factories. The Jews were the hard working people who made up most of the business owners, lawyers, doctors, and educated people. As a German in 1938, you had to be with the Nazis, and against the Jews; or be an outsider and be run over by the Nazi machine. The first thing Nazi's outlawed against Jew's were their rights to own firearms, and they confiscated them, prior to the day they rounded them up and took them away the rest of their property. The normal German's (the sheep of the day) watched, scared to say or do anything. I am sure they thought "I don't want to have my property taken like them, and therefore I will not say anything." Like Hitler, Bob is busy on television using sympathetic means to take away your firearms. He uses shootings such as the attack on the Charleston AME Zion Church, to justify taking away weapons. If nothing is done, $2^{nd}$ Amendment Rights will be taken away next, with the screaming of racism if you are against it. Our rights as American's given to us by God led men and women, are about to be taken away because we think it is insignificant, and it won't bother me. What will come after our weapons are taken away? What are the third and fourth order effects?

In Ferguson, Missouri, a loud mouth individual with a loud speaker screamed out that Police Officers are all racist in America, and that "we" African American's have gotten to show them. That something became burning down buildings, beating white people who are probably are like me and never think about racism, and looting stores like Wal-Mart. They were on television screaming how racist America was and that people like me were racist. And the televisions ate this up, as if it was part of their propaganda. As a white male, I was taken aback. I am not racist. I have had businesses and hired people of other races, and have no clue why they would be screaming like that. However, in introspect, I began to understand. Just like the apes that attacked to expand their territory, the African American males were banding to expand their territory, just like Bob would want and Hitler wanted. They preached violence to the white man to make up for the years of slavery that their ancestors had faced in the 1800's, like white people and Jews had never been enslaved. They preached that law enforcement was racist, and that black men were unfairly incarcerated more than twice the amount of white people, using no other statistics, and like white people were just sitting around trying to figure out how to put black people in jail for no reason. They never said anything about Michael Brown should not have stolen or that black people would not be in jail if they lived honest lives and followed the laws of the land and the Bible, because Bob did not see that as important. And then, which was a complete surprise, the President of the United States came on and talked about the sins of our country and the 1800's, like he was trying to help incite them to do what they were doing. Through speeches the President gave, instead of trying to bring us together, he was trying to incite more rioting, almost like Bob had written his speech for him. I noticed no

African American's spoke up because they would have been outside the group, and they would be attacked. The African American's, just like the Chimpanzee's, understood that there was territory being taken, and for them to say anything could put them in the cross hairs to be targeted, and they said nothing. And then, the follow on actions took place, which had to have been orchestrated by Satan himself. A dumb Police Officer shot a black man in a park in Charleston, South Carolina. And, then an evil white teen ager killed a group of black people in a church in Charleston, South Carolina. African American's got even more in a group, and the television talk shows lived on. Bob was living his glory days of American hatred of one another. "White people are racist against black people, but black people are not racist against white people," was the call of the day in newspapers and on television shows across America. As a white male wanting to be left alone, I became more concerned about myself and my family. I started questioning myself, because it seemed like the world thought I as a white, Judeo-Christian male was racist. I looked at African American's different at work, and started asking myself "is this person racist against white people?" I may be the only one putting this in writing, but I am not the only white person who wondered where this was going, as Facebook will attest. The President, like he was trying to urge the evil on, got on national television and kept using the word "nigger," and separated the white people from the black people even more, as if once again Bob had written his speech. I felt for the first time in the 48 years of my life that I was an outsider in my own country, and had no clue or faith in the leadership of this country that there was anyone that was looking for my best interest as a Judeo-Christian white male any more. I began to think, the government is going to re-build itself around these racist groups, and eventually weed out, kill and destroy white people who are living in this country. I did not want to think this. I wanted things to go back to normal. But, we are where we were. I was living in an outside group, waiting for the Chimpanzees to come attack me to get the little territory that I had. Laws are being changed by Judges now without approval of the largest percentage of the voters, through the use of judges, who with the help of Bob are able to make any laws they want. The attacks have begun on the 2nd Amendment. Is the ruling that American's cannot own guns coming soon? At that point, only criminals will own guns. How much power is in the hands of these people who claim to be the American government, but are in reality men who are redefining the definition of what an American is, while screaming racism? Where is the defined difference between right and wrong when they took my Bible and my Holy Scripture that this country was founded on, that my mother taught me right from wrong from, that I tried to teach my children right and wrong from, and said it is no longer a viable tool for our government. Where is the Senate, who are supposed to introduce Bills and then have them ratified by the Congress? Why is law like the Healthcare Plan and the Gay Marriage Plan being put into law by the Supreme Court instead of going in front of people who are supposed to represent me, and that I vote for? The Supreme Court Justices do not represent me, and I had no vote in who was put on that bench. The Supreme Court does whatever the sitting President and Bob want them to do. The country at this point is no longer in line with what America was made for. We fought a Revolutionary War against England for taxation without representation. And, the Bible has become racist? I am a racist because I believe in the Bible and its words? I am a racist because I question black men who burn down buildings and beat white American's?  America, in many aspects, is being torn at the seams by our own people, leaving a gaping hole for other governments to attack through.  Joseph Stalin is laughing in his grave.

## Chapter (11) You Are Joking, Right?

*In October 2009, a 15 year old girl was gang raped in a schoolyard during a Homecoming dance in California.  During 2.5 hours, Police state as many as 20 bystanders saw what was happening, and none came forward to help the girl, who was intoxicated.  She was assaulted both sexually and physically by several men.  It became a "check it out" type of thing, and young people from the dance went out to watch.  When the Police were finally called, the crowd ran and left the girl, just lying there.  One witness stated "They were kicking her in her head and they were beating her up, robbing her and ripping her clothes off; it's something you can't get out of your mind.  I saw people, like, dehumanizing her; I saw some pretty crazy stuff.  She was pretty quiet; I thought she was like dead for a minute, but then I saw her moving around.  I feel like I could have done something but I don't feel like I have any responsibility for anything that happened."*

On or about July 1, 2015 Donald Trump threw his hat in the ring to become the President of the United States.  Donald Trump is an unknown religious faith, alpha male who is able to beat his chest and show his territory.  As such, a lot of the other groups (apes) started to flock to him.  Some of them saw, hey this guy might beat me and take my territory if we don't side with him. Automatically his speeches began to go virulently against a weaker group, the Hispanics who are in our borders illegally, with the intentions of getting the other groups (apes) to get on board against them.  The weirdest part of all of this is that a lot of Hispanics work for Donald Trump, in his Casino's and buildings, throughout the world.  However, this attack worked well.  The African American's could see this as a chance to not be thought of as the group that is preaching racism, and its top leaders may even make money off Mr. Trump's campaign.  The whites saw this as a man preaching the economy and wealth, and are starting to flock to him for his supposed capability of building business.  There is no mention of God, or trying to follow his will.  The territory he is going after is the illegal Hispanics in America.  They will be the losers through this campaign.  To benefit Donald Trump, just like manna from heaven, a Hispanic individual who had been taken out of the US five times, came back in the US and killed a woman in California.  He became the new face of what was now wrong in America, and the groups, just like Apes, started focusing on the Hispanics as the weaker group, all televised by Bob for us to agree with.   The groups are being reset from a focus on whites being racist against black people and black people being racist against white people to where both groups are about to become racist against Hispanic people.  The group's dynamics changed in about 20 days.  It is amazing to see the dynamics as they shape the next Presidential election, just like it is to see who would be the next Chimpanzee leader in the jungle.

## Chapter (12) Apes Have No Soul

*On October 25, 1994 Susan Smith, a white female from Union, SC reported to Police that she had been carjacked and that her kids had been taken by a black man.  A few days later, she finally confessed that she had killed her kids by letting her Mazda Protégé sink in a lake, thus drowning them.  She allegedly did this so she could have a relationship with a wealthy man.*

Men are becoming much like apes because they have no soul. Many men and women could kill another man or woman for something as simple as $10 to buy crack with, and they don't care and have no further thought about it after the act has occurred. The destruction of man's souls has come about for several reasons, including the absence of teaching the Bible or any moral code in public schools, the destruction of the church by its own leaders, and the spreading of atheism by the world.

The savior of liberating schools from teaching the Bible was Madilyn Murray O'Hair, the leader of the American atheist movement, who was kidnapped, murdered, and mutilated along with her son, John Garth Murray and granddaughter Robin Murray O'Hair by a fellow member of her American Atheist group, so he could steal her money. This is in line with what atheism is all about, survival of the fittest. Atheism matters not if you lie, cheat, steal or kill because in the end you are going to die. This is the summation of what is taught to most kids in school.

The Judeo-Christian church is under attack. I want to say it is primarily from the world, but it requires no outside enemy. Satan is willing to work as well inside of the church as outside, and he loves to divide and conquer, like any trained General. In the normal church, all it takes is one disturbing rumor to float around, and it will usually divide a church. Or, have a Deacon stand in front of the church, like I saw one time, who talked about how he did not believe in a part of the Bible, and "voila" you have a split church. It could be something as simple as Paul's words, like where he said a woman should not speak in church, or should cover their head in a church, and you could have people running for the door.  Why?  Because people want to believe what they want to believe instead of humbling themselves and taking the Bible at face value, and searching for meaning, like the Berean's did.   We human beings have a problem seeking God's will, and are usually always seeking our own will.

Finally, the world is spreading atheism faster and faster.  No one ever slows down to ask "hey, where did the first matter come from?"  It is easy to just discount it all and believe the world just magically appeared.  Then, you add in a little Charles Darwin, spreading the words that the world just evolved, and you have men and women running around like apes, worrying little about their soul or their afterlife.  Everyone just begins to believe, "well, we have no soul.  We are just born and then we die."  There is no intelligent designer or God in heaven.  And the sheep watching television just believe it and travel in masses to believe what is put out.   We want to be cool like the guy on television.

The soul is the center piece of the works of Jesus Christ.  When we give our life to him, we are re-born, and our soul becomes destined to be with him in heaven.  We are given living water.  The body surely will die and decay, but the soul will live forever.  An ape has no knowledge of such, and has never thought of a soul; like many men and women are beginning to do in the modern age of "survival of the fittest."  A dead body is no longer anything but a shell.  The soul has travelled to what Paul calls the third heaven, to be judged by our heavenly maker.

### Chapter (13) Apes Have a Need to be in the Jungle to Survive

*Bernard Madoff made huge amounts of money off the greed of his investors. He promised huge interest on investment money, and swindled millions from people he knew. When he was finally arrested on December 11, 2008, he had committed the largest financial fraud in US history. The estimated amount of actual losses is valued at $18 billion. His children (and it was suspected his banker) knew what he was doing, but none said anything until he was prosecuted.*

An ape needs to live in a jungle, where he is hidden behind the trees and growth. The same is true with Judeo-Christianity. We Judeo-Christians, with our Bible's and talking about God's word, make those who are "normal" feel uncomfortable. When we start talking about God's laws, we start having people who are Gay feel threatened, and they want to either fight or flee. God's law is uncomfortable and threatening. It always has been. Jesus was crucified. John the Baptist was beheaded. Paul was banned to an island then later killed. Stephen was stoned. Many even wanted to stone Moses. Many Homosexuals and other sinners still try to state they believe in God and want to follow God's laws, but not this or that certain law. Unfortunately, Judeo-Christians are the same way. God said not to eat pork, but the first lunch you go to at your average Baptist Church is a Barbeque. When asked about it, Christians always quote Peter "rise and kill and eat," as the reason we can now eat pork. Or they quote Paul, who argued that we should no longer be under the law, although Jesus never said he came to change the law. However, we humans are a little more complex than that. We are hypocrites. We preach adhering to the Ten Commandments, but then abolish the Sabbath because we no longer believe in it, for no good reason besides the Disciples picked corn on the Sabbath and Jesus healed. Jesus never said to abolish the Sabbath. In fact, his mother respected the Sabbath by waiting till it was over to go to his tomb. Because true Judeo-Christians believe in all of God's laws, they threaten "normal" people, who want to see Judeo-Christians run off and quietened. The normal people take the "Ten Commandments" out of courtrooms, although they would like to see a witness tell the truth, the whole truth and nothing but the truth so help them God. The "normal" people don't think of justice until something happens to them, and then they want immediate justice, like the Chicago protestors did in Ferguson, Missouri. They do not care for our rules of law and our court system, and they just will burn down a Papa John's Pizza or mass loot a Wal-Mart if the laws don't bend their way. They are just trying to expand their territory, like a Chimpanzee would do.

### Chapter (14) Churches Need Policing Too

*In the 1980's, it became widely known that Priests, Nuns and others in the Catholic Church had molested boys and girls for a long time, and Priests had been moved to other locations to cover it up. One individual was quoted as saying "the crisis in the United States reached epidemic proportions within the Church, the likes of which haven't been witnessed before." In 2004, the John Jay report computed that 4,392 Priests and Deacons had allegations made against them. How, out of all of these abused kids, did no one report this to the Police, or were we just so blind we did not want to see? And, of those who are truly guilty, did they not listen to the words in the Bible that they worked with?*

We Judeo-Christians have gotten to come to the realization that to remain active in our faith, we may be forced to worship more in our homes and amongst ourselves instead of in organized churches, especially if we are going to keep our entire faith in the Bible. Organized religion in churches and synagogues is becoming a watered down version of the truth, designed not to offend anyone, and does not follow all the laws in the Bible as handed down by God. Furthermore, the Preachers that is in the pulpit sometimes shy from the word so as not to offend anyone.

So, welcome to the Church. You don't believe me now, but it is coming. There will come a day when you will worship God in Spirit and truth, and will not need the walls of the church. I know, you are sitting in your house or on your porch reading and it does not seem like Church. But, the truth is, you are the closest right now to church as you will ever get in your own home. The arguments are already rising in your head, including my home is not a church, I miss the people in my church, and if I go to church at home, where will I be buried at? The questions are infinite, and I do not have all the answers. But, if you are going to church and are miserable, are afraid of being attacked like an ape outside of his tribe, not learning things, seeing things that disagree with the Bible, don't feel safe, and don't feel led by God, why not try Church at home (but not by television). Church at home is by praying and reading the King James Version of the Bible on your own, and seeking God's knowledge. As the world continuously turns toward Satan through Hollywood and television news networks, you might find your safest place to serve, focus, and relate with God is in your home, away from the jungle of organized services. Furthermore, you might be surprised what you get out of it.

Everything I will discuss with you is Biblically based, unlike the Gay Episcopalian Minister.

I believe completely in the Bible. I have been reading through the entire Bible at least once a year over the last nine years, and as I study and pray, I see fundamental differences between what is being preached in the Church and what the Bible says. And, I see the survival of the fittest mentality and jungle attitude often associated with the interior of churches. It could often make anyone feel uncomfortable, especially if you are just seeking a church to worship God in. Often, during a sermon, a Pastor will seek one verse and stick with that verse, although there is another part of the Bible that contradicts it. He does not discuss the Bible in its entirety, to give you the seeker the knowledge to make informed and God filled decisions, and therefore, cuts short the word of God. As I visit Churches throughout the United States, there are fundamental differences in teaching God's word because Pastor's are afraid of offending someone, and are more interested in serving the world than God. They are like the Chimpanzee's; a member of a group, and want to stay in the group for fear of being attacked. Therefore, if you are at church just with yourself or your family, you have no one to offend. And, as time goes on, and the country continues to be taken over by evil men and women, which will happen until the end of time, you can worship freely at any given time. And, you can be dual purposed; worshipping at home as often as possible, but still going to church if and when possible.

This freedom to worship in our homes was given to us from Jesus. Remember when Jesus was killed in the Bible. Prior to his murder, which was brought about by evil Jewish people and Romans led by Satan, he said in John 2:19 "destroy this temple and I will raise it again in three days." Prior to this, in Matthew 2:12-22, one of the first public works that Jesus worked on was the temple where covetous Priests and rulers made the Church into a market place and a place for trading currency, much like a Baptist Church I know of in Vienna, Virginia which does not have a Wednesday night church service, but has a "pay a fee" Pizza dinner and financial management workshop. I know this because I accidentally visited, sat at a table and expected to hear a sermon or Wednesday night service, and was told I had to pay my fee to stay in a Baptist Church. I left because I did not want to hear a life insurance salesman; but what if I wanted to stay, and did not have my fee? Is that what Jesus had in mind for a church? In my mind, and I may be wrong, but at that point, the church had become a house of merchandise; and people are flocking to this instead of focusing on worshipping God. We are all distracted, and have way too many electronic devices and duties taking away from our focus on God the Father, his son Jesus, the Holy Ghost, and the Bible, the guidebook to life. Furthermore, Jesus is the personal Savior we were given to be able to approach the Father with Prayer, without having to go through a Priest at a church or temple, and give a sacrifice, like occurred in the Old Testament. This means you can go to prayer to the Lord in your house right now, and he is listening. Stop a minute and pray the Lord's Prayer with me: "Our Father, who art in heaven, hallowed be thy name, thy kingdom come, thy will be done, on the earth as it is on heaven. Give us this day, our daily bread, and forgive us our trespasses, as we forgive those who trespass against us. And lead us not into temptation, but deliver us from evil. For thou is the kingdom, the power and the glory forever. Amen."

And, Jesus further went on to say in Matthew 6:6 that when you pray, go into your room, close the door, and pray to your

Father who is unseen. Then your Father, who sees what is done in secret, will reward you. Since he said your room, I don't know any place better to have Church service than with yourself, your family, and God in "your room." Your home is the perfect place.

I have been in Churches throughout the United States, and even overseas over the last few years. I have seen some really good churches that are on fire for the Lord (especially in South Korea). And I have seen Preachers go through an entire sermon and not mention God, Jesus, or the Holy Spirit (especially around Washington, DC). One Preacher I sat through one time talked about his personal experiences with no known connotation to God for over 40 minutes, during a church service. I kept wondering if he really thought we wanted to hear about this, and I would have personally been more entertained if he read "Green Eggs and Ham" instead of trying to tell stories with no moral values or that relate to God's experience in his life. As a man struggling to maintain a God focused and centered life and still failing, I need to hear the word in a way that can bring me closer to God. During times like this, I usually just bring and read my own Bible during Church services.

God leads men and women in the path that he wants them to go in. If you feel led to try something new because of circumstances in your church, try worshipping at home. If this does not work for you then go find a church. But, let's get back to God and let's ensure you are saved and ready to go to heaven. Let me ask you this. Have you been saved by the blood of Jesus? If not, pray this simple prayer with me. "Father God, please forgive me of all of my sins. I know and understand that I am a sinner in need of a Savior, and accept Jesus Christ as this Savior. I trust Jesus Christ as my Lord. I ask you for forgiveness of my sins, and request that I am worthy of entering your kingdom." Congratulations, if you were not saved, you are now if you sincerely prayed that prayer. This is the first part of your salvation, and it is easy. And, I have found that I need to add "Lord, help my unbelief," as often I am not sure I have the belief that is needed to get into the Kingdom of heaven on my own.

Now, here is where truth becomes reality, and it is a little harder, but you can do it if you try. If you prayed that prayer right now or any time in the past, have you changed your life to mirror Jesus, who never sinned? This is how you can really tell if a person is saved, as quoted by Jesus himself at the end of John 8:1-11. He states, "Jesus returned to the Mount of Olives, but early the next morning he was back again at the Temple. A crowd soon gathered, and he sat down and taught them. As he was speaking, the teachers of religious law and the Pharisees brought a woman who had been caught in the act of adultery. They put her in front of the crowd. Teacher, they said to Jesus, this woman was caught in the act of adultery. The law of Moses says to stone her. What do you say? They were trying to trap him into saying something they could use against him, but Jesus stooped down and wrote in the dust with his finger. They kept demanding an answer, so he stood up again and said, all right, but let the one who has never sinned throw the first stone. Then he stooped down again and wrote in the dust. When the accusers heard this, they slipped away one by one, beginning with the oldest, until only Jesus was left in the middle of the crowd with the woman. Then Jesus stood up again and said to the woman, where are your accusers, didn't even one of them condemn you. No Lord, she said. And Jesus said, neither do I. Go and sin no more."

This last statement to me is the most important statement that Jesus ever said. He had just saved her. She was forgiven of all her transgressions, primarily by Jesus, but also by a group of Jewish men that were about to stone her. Her life was spared and she could continue to live on this earth. But, Jesus last statement was so powerful, "go and sin no more." She was forgiven her sins for now. She was saved. But, she needed to go and attempt to live life from that point without sin to the best of her ability.

When we are saved, we often forget this. We get saved, are on fire with the Lord, but have to live around other human beings and family members who often invoke the worst in us. It can seem like our lives are a modern day war. Modern day churches often teach a doctrine that you can be saved and can do anything you want. In fact, at least one doctrine teaches that the more you sin, the more you have grace. Some teach that Jesus came to give us "freedom" or "liberty" from the law. It is my opinion that this is incorrect. It is also modern doctrine in the churches that you can be saved, and pick and choose which words of God or Jesus you want to follow. Once again, this is incorrect. As you read the Bible, I hope you are convinced to build a life around following every tenant of the Bible, especially as given to us from God and Jesus. We are fools to do anything else. The Bible is a perfect guidebook, and is the book designed to give us both a better life here on earth, and in the afterlife. And, if we are going to Police our society, then we need to learn to Police ourselves. The Bible is the greatest book ever for us to learn how to Police ourselves.


Terrorized

*George Washington was with General George Braddock when they were ambushed during the French and Indian War. General Braddock died of wounds. George Washington escaped with little injuries, although he has two horses shot out from under him and four bullets pass through his coat. He goes on to lead the Continental Army through the Revolutionary War, and to become the First President of the United States.*

I often hear men who are "Airborne" in the Army talk about how great they were able to jump out of airplanes, and how they are not scared of anything. I too have jumped out of airplanes, but every time I did I was scared until my Parachute opened. Then, I would laugh like a school girl. I was scared, and have been scared in other circumstances of life also. I believe fear is a natural feeling, especially when life and death are involved. For a man or woman to say they never have been scared, it probably wrong unless they were born with a physical or mental deformity.

However, it is possible I believe with God's help, for a man to remain completely calm in the face of calamity. For example, as a Police Officer, I and others was shot at by a man with a pistol from only a few feet away. We ran from an apartment we were in with him, as he shot his pistol at us from short range, missing us only because of God's intervention. As I turned around to face him, when he came out the door toward us, I felt the most calm I had ever felt, and almost was laughing at his pointing the pistol and firing at me, and me returning fire. Only God can give me this type of calm, as it definitely is not innate to my soul. I remember thinking "I should be scared," but instead was laughing. It was strange, and can only be explained that God or his angels was convincing me that I was alright. We wound up wounding him, arresting him, and he was later charged and convicted with 18 counts of attempted murder.

I have felt this in other places also. When I was in the National Guard stationed in Iraq, I was leading a convoy back toward a base when I saw a group of birds flying directly toward my vehicles in a "V" formation. I knew something was not right from that, and a couple of minutes later my convoy was hit by an Improvised Explosive Device (IED), left on the side of the road by some Iraqi who wanted us dead. No one was directly hit by this munition because of God's grace; but we could have been. We Soldiers stood on the side of the road looking at all the Iraqi civilians who had gathered to look, with the full knowledge that someone (probably more than one) in that crowd had wanted us dead. But, I remember feeling calm. Like, God was watching over us, as we got back in our vehicles and continued heading toward our base. The front of a truck was damaged, and a couple of Soldiers had hearing injuries, but other than that we were alright.

Only God can give a person peace in the middle of trials. A woman I go to church with had a daughter who committed suicide. She loved her daughter very much, and was very hurt by this. Her daughter was a lawyer, accomplished and probably one of the smartest people in North Carolina. She had written Prosecution Codes still used by courts in North Carolina today. However, the woman, who is also our piano player, came to church the next week and assumed her position as our piano player. She had to be hurting inside, but I could tell that she was even more concerned about making sure we had a piano player in church, than sitting on a pew having people feel sorry for her. She became my hero; after all, who could handle the death of a child like that? She was so strong because of her strong faith in the Lord, and that she would see her daughter again.

While we are on earth, we are destined to become terrorized. Whether it is from armed militants funded by Iran to further the Islamic territory, or from evil leaders in high places who are wolves but wear sheep clothing, we Judeo-Christian's are destined to be terrorized. We always have been. In Rome, Judeo-Christians were blamed for everything. Rome used to crucify all of its enemies, and there would be roads just lined up with dying or dead enemies of the Roman State being crucified. Rome, a nation that was built on the belief in Pagan God's and their rulings, was innately against Judeo-Christians. While some rulers were tolerant, other allowed citizens to murder Judeo-Christians and offer their blood to Pagan idols.

I do not know where our nation is going. The United States was built and had intense growth from being a Judeo-Christian and giving nation. Over the last few years, under evil leaders who wear sheep's clothing, the country has been eradicated into a mess of survival of the fittest citizens with limited freedoms, and dependency of welfare and government programs. Where we as a country used to give and give freely, our giving is now dependent on Franklin Graham's Samaritan's Purse and Operation Blessing, and other Christian organizations to really help out. It can seemingly only get worse, especially for the Judeo-Christian. Oh you can hide behind the façade of trying to be a friendlier and gentler country, but in reality it is the Judeo-Christians who will be attacked. The individuals who are atheist can lie to each other and to the government and it does not bother them. They will lie about how much money they make, and not pay taxes, and it is no big deal. Judeo-

Christians know they are under the watching eye of God. They will not lie about what they make, and therefore they will turn in honest wages. The Judeo-Christians will be taxed more than the atheist's. It is just going to happen. Also, the Judeo-Christian's will be persecuted for not believing in homosexual marriage. It is one thing for the world to be homosexual, and just to do the acts. However, that is not enough. The United States Supreme Court has now come out and stated that Gay marriage is legal throughout the land. Marriage, a term spoken of in the Bible as between a man and woman, is being redefined by lawyers as between a girl and a girl. Thus a group of 21st century lawyers proudly and arrogantly stated that they are smarter than God and his laws. Therefore, for a church to turn down a gay marriage would be a strange strain against the Federal Government. Active churches may or not in the future be required to have Gay weddings, against the beliefs of the Judeo-Christian people in the church. After all, if you are saved, you want to follow God's laws, right? And God's law says that marriage is between a man and a woman, and not a man and a man. The Bible says for this a woman should leave her mother and father and join with her husband. Just the thought of a man marrying another man is retarded; but not to our Federal Government. The forms are even a lie, as one has to wrongly state they are the husband or the wife. The next thing is a man's marriage to his dog, car, or a child. Just like Rome, it dares God to act. Nero, a former Roman Emperor, married a child, and dared the citizens to say anything to him. The United States government, just like Rome did before the black plague killed millions in Rome, dares God to say anything to liberals that gay marriage is wrong. This is only the tip of where we are going next. Who cares that it was Adam and Eve in the garden, and that Eve was made for Adam so he should not be lonely. So what that God says it is an abomination for a man to lie with a man, as he should lie with a woman. The Supreme Court members are smarter than God, or at least they are now. The final judgement will not be from man, but from God. Let's see how smart they are then. It is my prayer I can be a fly on the wall as those members of the Supreme Court that redefined marriage meet God.

So, another reason to go to church at home is you don't have to be a member of a church that has a Gay wedding. The Gay wedding thing is really a small victory for Gay people. What is the large victory for them is that they got a statement that their way was right, and God's way was wrong. The Gay people are smarter than God, just like they were in Sodom and Gomorrah, before he destroyed the city. The God of heaven, who created the heavens and earth, and created man in his image, surely is taken aback by the pride and arrogance of Gay people marching around in Gay attire against his Bible, and the United States Supreme Court proudly stating they were smarter than God. One Gay parade in New Orleans had a 5 year old male boy in just a Speedo type bathing suit "twerking" as the marchers went by to celebrate. And, this was thought of as normal by the drunken gay revelers. The pedophile marriage will be next. Most people cannot see it, but it is coming, just like the fights to the death slowly evolved in Roman amphitheaters. It is a slippery slope we are on, all forecast by the Bible. Or the White House, aglow in the prideful colors of Gay symbolism, arrogantly stating that we, the United States of America, are going to do whatever we want because we are who we are. Bob sends our message throughout the world, that "we are the United States: you couldn't destroy us, like Rome, Nazi Germany, or the Persian Empire. We can do what we want. We are better than the other countries that were destroyed. We can never be destroyed!" LOL

American's are so foolish. God has given us warnings. He gave us two earthquakes in the same day on separate coasts of the United States in 2012. He has given us sudden fish and bird deaths. He has given us enemies on every side of the country. The Assyrian's, who have been a thorn in the sides of God's people throughout history, now have nuclear weapons. We have intense shark attacks on the Eastern Coast. Still, we feel somehow protected behind our modern technology and our stealth bombers and our anti-missile defense systems. This is so foolish. The only real defense we have in America is our faith in God, and his willingness to protect us. The reality is, as easy as it was for men to fly two planes into the World Trade Center and the Pentagon in 2001, is how easy it will be for Iran to get a nuclear bomb in the Long Beach, California Port Terminal, or for North Korea, Syria, and Iran to work together on a nuclear warhead that can be exploded over American cities by use of satellite and space technologies. We American's want to believe this has not happened so far because we are smart and have protected our borders. The truth is, our best defense is from a little widow woman in Marshville, North Carolina, who stays in prayer constantly and tends to take care of the others in her rural church. Or from an elderly, poor woman who attends church in St. Paul's, North Carolina. She barely has enough money to buy food to eat, but is worried about her friend who has Alzheimer's. Or, for an 83 year old man who lives in Lenoir, NC who gets bread, diapers, and other items from Operation Blessing and delivers it to the members of his church, even though he only has one arm. God does not destroy America for those praying elderly people, and the thousands of other poor ones like her who are praying for their children and this nation, even though her children and associates are riding as fast as possible toward hell. These elderly "saviors" are why God does not destroy the earth, and why there is still hope. AC-DC's song rings out in my head "I'm on the highway to hell…" As God was asked before he destroyed Sodom and Gomorrah, "would you destroy the city if it has ten good men?" God still has sympathy for the poor, the downtrodden, and those who are seeking him. Unfortunately, the destruction will happen before people get back on their knees. These elderly people, who still believe and have faith, are dying. The children who are entering this era of their lives do not have the same faith or hope in Jesus Christ.

Anyone in law enforcement or that have fought in wars know that intelligence is not all that matters on a battlefield. Things go wrong all the time, such as when Delta Force tried to go into Iran under the Jimmy Carter administration and wrecked a helicopter into a plane, killing soldiers. Or when Navy Seals went in to get Osama bin Laden and their helicopter went down. Or when I was leading a convoy in Baquaba, Iraq and my convoy was attacked, and my radio did not work. I could not contact anyone and was in the middle of nowhere. You plan for your contingencies. Modern technology, as great as it is, does not always work, especially when you need it the most. The greatest plans for contingencies in the Armed Forces are by military Chaplains, who are praying for the health, safety, and deliverance of soldiers as they go into war. I know of no soldiers who voluntarily want to go into battle with an atheist or blatant homosexual. As we true warriors know, and as Napoleon stated, the moral is to the physical as 3:1. In other words, we have a 3 to 1 greater chance of winning if we are the morally right peoples. When we go to war against an Army that is more morally correct than us, we will lose. This corrupt administration that is being put into office by falsifying election ballots and returns is destroying our country, and there is little that seemingly can be done about it, without being labelled "racist." And, there will be other false elections in the United States most likely from today through the end of time. Through civilian military leadership that is selected by this current administration, we will soon see our military losing in the war on terror and in other upcoming battles unless something is done. The moral is to the physical as 3:1. We used to never back down. The US military will begin to look weak as we go forward, as planned by Bob's agenda. The civilian and top military leaders will reflect this Satanic administration, and will follow their orders, to the detriment of the normal Soldier.

Oh, you can go back through history and look at the Battles God has had his hands in. For example, in 1814 at the Battle of New Orleans, the English had a superior Army and Navy attacking an American defense, led by Andrew Jackson or "Old Hickory" and made up of Indians, Pirates, Marines, the Tennessee militia, free black men, and other individuals who were promised money and 160 acres of land to fight. And, they fought and won, against the British who outnumbered them by almost ten times. At the end of the Battle of New Orleans, which ended the War of 1812 and British aggression against America, over 2000 British soldiers were killed. Only 13 American soldiers died. It would take an awful skewed man or woman to say that God's hand was not involved in the Battle of New Orleans, or that his blessing was not on "Old Hickory."

God is there. He wants you to focus on him in spirit and in truth. He does not want you bogged down in problems in your church that distract from why you go. Therefore, you can worship God in the peace and tranquility of your home, away from the wolves that are ready to pray on you, and with a renewed focus on the spirit. Even in the church, there are those wolves that are ready to pray on the weak. I have seen them attack elderly women, who have problems taking care of themselves, and are willing to give everything they have away. I have even seen a coup in a Baptist Church, to where when the preacher got in the pulpit and was elected preacher, and then he stayed there for 18 years, against the people in the church who soon found out he brought his mistress piano player to the church, who he had an affair with throughout the time in the church, and before he came. Evil is everywhere, and the church is not immune. While there are great churches with great people, there are some bad churches, which do not do God, Jesus, or the Holy Spirit justice on earth.

In the Bible, it speaks that the frequent and fervent prayer of a righteous man (or woman) availeth much. I completely believe it does. However, it often takes a form not seen of the person praying. The almighty God often moves in mysterious ways that we human beings cannot understand. During the time of the Roman occupation throughout Europe, Asia, Africa, and including Israel, men looked for a savior that would come in and save them. They looked for a man who would cause an uprising and cause the people to rise up and to get rid of the invaders. They did not see a gentle man, riding a donkey, coming into the village, speaking softly of peace and forgiving thy enemies. No one could have seen this, unless they were angelic beings themselves. Jesus came to forgive. His kingdom was not of this earth at that time, but will be in the future. We are so focused on this earth, to where we forget that there is another world to come. If you ever look at a body after death, you can tell it was never anything but a shell. The soul has left. Jesus said he goes to prepare a place for you, if it was not so he would not say so. This earth is not it. Churches today rarely talk of heaven or hell, but they are real places. We, when we die, are going to one of them. It is going to happen. The earth is merely a training ground for what is to come. Today's churches often talk of things not even in the Bible, such as the acceptance of homosexuality. In Ezekiel 22:28, it states, "And her prophets have daubed them with untempered mortar, seeing vanity, and divining lies to them, saying, Thus said the Lord GOD, when the LORD has not spoken." Ezekiel 22:28 I cannot tell you enough; read your Bible and interpret the words yourself. God will speak to you the truth.

## Chapter (15) Good and Evil

*"That book (Bible), sir, is the rock on which our Republic rests." Andrew Jackson, who was also known as Old Hickory, was the 7th President of the US and a hero of the Battle of New Orleans.*

The God of all times is in charge of both good and evil. We see this time and time again in the Bible, where God puts evil government administrations over his people, because they have turned their backs on God. And, we can see this in history and even today, as we have in power one of the most corrupt and evil administrations (at least as far as in relation to the Bible) that has ever been in power. Judges who do not seek justice but money and power; Senator's reduced to babbling; and a President who seems destined to destroy this country that we have worked so hard to build, so that he can impress Bob, who paid for his campaign from Hungary. Clear previous examples of this is when Nebuchadnezzar was able to take over Israel, the Israeli's were put in slavery in Egypt, and while not in the Bible, how Hitler rose to power to ensnare and kill the Jews at the beginning of World War II.

Nebuchadnezzar laid seize to Israel around 586 B.C. During the siege, God was against Israel, and about everything the Jewish people did to try to keep from being enslaved went wrong. The King of Jerusalem, Zedekiah, watched with his own eyes his sons being killed. Then, he was blinded and taken prisoner in Babylon until his death. After the fall of Jerusalem, Solomon's temple was destroyed and the city was annihilated. The people of Israel who were not killed were taken to Babylon as slaves. They remained under Nebuchadnezzar, until he became aware (through becoming crazy enough to live in a field and eat grass) that there was only one God, and that he (Nebuchadnezzar) was only King because of this God.

The enslavement of the Israelites under the Egyptian people was not so clear in coming. There was no battle, just a slow evolvement to where the people became slaves. It all happened after Joseph had saved his people from famine, and his brothers came to live with him in Egypt. Eventually, this blessed generation died, as well as the Pharaoh that had given them the land and cattle to thrive. After this, a new king came to the throne, and he cared none for Israel, or its ways and its people. He chose to forget all about what Joseph had previously done for Egypt (saved it from starvation and raised it financially), and took action against the growing number of Israeli foreigners (Hebrews) living in Egypt. Pharaoh limited the personal freedoms of the Hebrews, and then enslaved them with high taxes. The children of Israel soon became enslaved, living in forced labor camps to build cities, erect monuments, construct roads, and hew stones to make brick and tile. When the new king saw that the Israelis continued to grow even while enslaved, he ordered the male babies to be thrown in the Nile River when they were born. The only group of Jews to escape this torment was the Levis, who did not mix with the Egyptians and were still in the favor of God. The remaining Israelis were enslaved for almost 400 years, until Moses led them to freedom by the directions of God.

Finally, we get to the next tragic chapter of the Jewish people, not written about in the Bible, but possibly forecast, through the writings of the prophets. This torture comes about less than 80 years ago, through the rise of a man named Adolph Hitler.

After the fall of the Roman Empire, Jewish merchants spread throughout the world, and were blessed beyond mention. They played a leading role in trade, merchandise, and finance all around the globe. In Leviticus 26:33 it states "I will scatter you among the nations." However, the most direct conviction of the Jews is in Leviticus 26:14 where it states, "but if you don't obey me, and do not observe all these Commandments, I will set my face against you, and you shall be defeated by your enemies. Those who hate you shall reign over you, and you shall flee when no one pursues you. And I will bring a sword against you that will execute the vengeance of the covenant, when you are gathered together within your cities. I will send pestilence amongst you, and you shall be delivered into the hands of the enemy." However, God said that he would never forget them, in Jeremiah 3:11 where it states "for I am with you, sayeth the Lord. To save you though I make a full end of all nations where I have scattered you, yet will I not make a complete end of you."

It is my opinion that the largest sin that befell the Jewish people between the end of the Roman empire and the rise of Adolph Hitler is that of usury, followed by organized prostitution rings (adultery). There were many Jewish bankers scattered throughout Europe by the rise of Adolph Hitler, and they had loaned money to the Czar of Russia and to other Kings. However, the Bible clearly states "If though lend money to any of my people, even to the poor with thee, there shalt not be to him as a creditor; neither shalt you charge upon him interest." In Leviticus 25:36 it states, "take thou no interest of him, or increase, but fear thy God, that thy brother may live with thee." In Leviticus 25:37 it states, "thou shalt not give him thy money upon interest, nor give him thy victuals for increase." In Deuteronomy 23:21 it states "unto a foreigner thou may lend upon interest, but unto thy brother thou shalt not lend upon interest, that the Lord thy God may bless thee in all that thou put thy hand unto, in the land wherest thou go to possess it." In Ezekiel 18:17 it states "That hath withdrawn his hand from the poor, that hath not receive interest on income, hath executed mine ordinances, hath walketh in my statutes; he shalt not die for the inequity of his father; he shalt surely live. "

After the fall of the Roman empire, Jewish banks continued to grow in prominence. Mosche Ameseth Rothschilds established one of the most powerful financial empires that the Jews ever possessed. Other prominent bankers also helped the German government with loans. However, after World War I, people in Germany were very poor, and the Jewish people still seemed to do well, collecting money from loans, and foreclosing on properties that were not paid on. Although the Jews were never much more than 1% of the German population between World War I and World War II, they owned 150 banks in 1923. In 1938, when Hitler started taking away rights of Jews, almost 85% of the brokers who worked in the Berlin Stock Market were Jewish. Also, 75% of the Doctors and 75% of the Lawyers were Jewish. Many of the hotels in Germany were Jewish owned, and they rented out the rooms by the hour for Jewish working prostitutes.

While there is no Bible or theological book that states that the Jewish people were persecuted in 1938 because of their excessive usury and other possible sins, there is a question raised. Never in the history of the world have a people been so persecuted. The Jewish people were actually burned in gasoline fueled buildings, and the German people did not do anything about it. The German people, so called "Christians" just looked the other way as their Jewish brethren were taken to cinder block buildings and burned to death. One German woman interviewed after the war, said she thought something odd but assumed they were cooking hogs and that was the smell. The human capacity to kill cannot be so great to where the souls of these men leading these Jewish people to their deaths were not affected, unless they were directly being guided by God himself as Nebuchadnezzar was? While we will never know until we are in heaven, it makes us wonder about the lessons learned.

Are the sins in America so thick to where God is leading our people toward an episode like the Jewish people had at the beginning of World War II? I ask this because of the way we have allowed evil to permeate and even lead our society, from the top ranks, and even in our government agencies. Have you ever owed money to the US Internal Revenue Service and had to pay the exurbanite interest that they charge. It, without a doubt, is the highest interest charged in the land, and usually to poor people who would pay their taxes if they had the money. It is so ludicrous to charge the poorest people extra usury because they cannot pay their taxes. Could our rights be taken away like those of the Jewish people? The first thing that was taken away from them (Jews) was their right to own firearms. What is the number one priority of the liberal Chicago driven Democratic party? Take our firearms. The Jewish people were slandered among the other people by being called racist. What do we see happening in America today? The most "racist" race (blacks) calling white people racists when they do not get what they want. Wake up! God will let this happen if you don't turn around this sinful nation that is stinking with sin, and fall on your knees. God will not help us once the punishment begins, until he believes it is enough. Wake up! Cinder Block built buildings with gasoline induced burnings of bodies. That was for the Jews. What will be given to the country that supports Gay Marriage and the abortions of millions of babies?

Finally, the Lord throughout Biblical time, and even today, has used Assyria as "the rod of mine anger" (Isaiah 10:5) to punish his people. Israel has been in the captivity of Assyria throughout history, and their leaders were violent men. Assyrian rulers have been infamous for their wickedness, and have flayed men alive and papered city walls with men's skins. Ashunasirpal (858-854BC) even pulled a rope through an Arab king's jaw, and chained him like a watchdog at a city gate. The Assyrian kings throughout history described themselves as Lions crushing their enemies. Once, I went to a palace formerly owned by Saddam Hussein. Inside the castle was a couch allegedly given to him by Yasser Arafat, the former leader of the Palestinian Leadership Organization (PLO). The couch had a Lion head, and the arm rests were hand carved wood into Lions paws. God uses good and evil to accomplish his will. Right now, he is using Assyria again against us, through Iranian backed organizations such as the Islamic State of Iraq and Syria (ISIS), Hezbollah, Hamas, and other organizations. These entities appear on the surface to be loosely controlled, but in reality are parts of the Lions reach of Iran or modern day Assyria toward the destruction of Israel and the United States of America.

So, we are where we are.  We are American's, living in a world dictated by "Bob," financed by a billionaire from Hungary, and perplexed on where we go from here.  We have kids who have been taught that drugs and the "world" provide the answers, and that the Bible is wrong.  What can we do?

**Chapter (14):** Put wayward Kids to Work and Teach Them Discipline and Who God Is.

*In the 1920's through the 1940's, the theory of eugenics was rampantly taught in colleges throughout the world, and discussed by the top minds in the scientific community.  The theory was that the best human beings were not breeding as rapidly as inferior human beings.  Included in these inferior human beings were foreigners, immigrants, Jews, degenerates, the "unfit," the feeble minded, and sick people.  As late as 1939, the Rockefeller Foundation supported research about this in Germany.*

**USNORTHCOM, in Conjunction with the National Guard Bureau and the US Coast Guard, should replace the Department of Homeland Security, and Utilize Current Department of Homeland Security Funding to Expand Already Existing Youth Challenge Academies for all Children (Ages 14-19) Who Become In Trouble with Law Enforcement and/or Drop/Fail Out of High School in the US and its Territories.** If we could do this one thing, just make compulsory military service a requirement instead of jail, we would teach kids some skills that would keep them off the streets and away from the Demonic forces that the world offers.  Furthermore, we could teach them values that include not being racist against each other.

**The following are some Facts Concerning Why We Need to Relook at Incarceration for Children ages 14-19:**

- College age youths are abusing a number of prescription medications, over the counter drugs, alcohol, cold medicine, OxyContin and medical marijuana. According to a Columbia University Study, 25% of college age kids have a problem with substance abuse or dependence, including taking Adderall to increase concentration.
- In 2010, almost 70,000 children or teenagers were put in jail or juvenile detention per day.
- Putting kids in juvenile detention reduces the chance that a student will ever graduate from high school by 13%, and raises the chances that the student will end up in jail by 22%.
- Fellow inmates today teach kids how to perform crime, join radical organizations, and even how to disarm and kill Police Officers.
- The United States currently spends approximately $6 billion on juvenile corrections each year.
- One out of three black males will go to prison at some point in their life, compared to one in six Latino males and one in seventeen white males.
- There were twenty-seven (27) Baltimore City Prison Guards which were involved in smuggling of drugs and cell phones for the Black Guerrilla Family gang in 2013, including at least 3 female prison guards who got pregnant by the same inmate at the prison. Other prisons, while not showing corruption on this scale, have had large lapses in moral conduct by both prison guards and wardens.
- Over 4 out of 10 prisoners released return to state prison within three years of their release.
- Moral values, such as described by the Bible, are no longer being taught to inmates, and therefore many still do not know right from wrong even when they are released. Right versus wrong is in many of their minds what crimes they can commit without getting caught.

**Facts on Why We Need to Increase the Size and Fighting Power of our Infantry, Utilizing Drafted Teenagers over the Next Twenty Years.**

- South Korea, and therefore, by default the US, is technically still at War with a nuclear North Korea.
- Nuclear weapons are available in North Korea, Soviet Union, Iran (we pretend not), Syria, India, Pakistan, Ukraine, and other countries throughout Europe.
- Islamic Fundamentalists, Homegrown Violent Extremists, and Mentally Ill individuals will continue to perform murder against US citizens within the border of the US, and in our interests overseas in the name of Jihad or for other sundry reasons.
- Nuclear and Atomic technology is becoming common knowledge among nations.
- The objectives of the Iranian Revolution of 1979 support terrorist organizations including Hezbollah in Lebanon, the Houthis in Yemen, Boko Haram and Al-Shabaab in Africa.
- The United States, Canada, England, France, Germany, and Israel are committed partners in the fight on terrorism.
- Russia has and will continue to spy on the United States, and will continue to conduct espionage operations on the United States, its citizens, and its allies.
- Russia freely uses its military industrial complex to manufacture and sell weapons to any country willing to pay the price.
- Economic devastation in China, Russia, North Korea, or other countries could trigger a nuclear war that wipes out large parts of our military requiring additional troops.
- It is with a high probability that Iran is working on obtaining more nuclear weapons, and that it has a working relationship in building nuclear capabilities with North Korea, Pakistan, Syria, and Russia.

- It is with a high probability that Iran already possesses at least one nuclear device of unknown strength or capacity.
- Of the approximately 68 million citizens of Iran, the largest majority are Shiite Muslims who believe a 12th Imam as a Messiah, will return and lead them. Many believe he cannot return until the Persian Empire is re-established, or the Silk Road Route. Therefore, through force, Iran will help pay Hezbollah, the Houthis, the Islamic State of Iraq and the Levant, Al Shabaab, Boko Haram, Los Zetas, and anyone else who will come to the table, money obtained legally and illegally to help spread the Shiite Muslim religion throughout the Middle East from India to Africa, which is nested with the fundamentals of the Islamic Revolution of 1979.
- It is with a high probability that when the Islamic Revolution spreads through Pakistan and India, currently controlled nuclear weapons will fall into the hands of Iranian puppet states (Houthis, Hezbollah, Boko Haram, Al Shabaab, Los Zetas), and will go to sale for the highest bidder.
- North Korea has the objectives to be able to launch nuclear war heads via Intercontinental Ballistic Missiles (ICBM), guide them over the US, bring them back into the Stratosphere via satellite, and detonate them near major cities. Instability, such as food shortages and social chaos, could prompt North Korea to launch Nuclear capabilities.
- Russia is continuing to work from Cold War Era Operations Orders, specifically written to impede the moral values and spirituality of the United States of America, thus causing the country to implode from within.[1]

---

[1] Most people do not even recognize what is at stake in the Global War on Terrorism (GWOT) with respect to American freedom and democracy. Just like the cold war, the stakes in the long war are high.

- China will continue to conduct cyber espionage in order to gain access to our most critical computer systems and our Supervisory Control and Data Acquisition (SCADA) systems which control our dams, bridges, power grids, and other systems.
- The 54 states and territories of the National Guard, which is managed by the National Guard Bureau, has the resources to act rapidly in virtually any place within the US, Guam, Virgin Islands, and Puerto Rico to support Homeland Defense, Homeland Security, and counter cyber activities.

**It is my sincere belief** that United States Northern Command (USNORTHCOM), in conjunction with the National Guard Bureau and the US Coast Guard should take over the functions of the Department of Homeland Security with oversight by Congress, to increase the security of the nation and to narrow the command and control needed for rapid response.

This re-assignment of roles would help to facilitate existing working relationships with local and state Police Departments, jails and juvenile systems, and as well as with other Federal agencies.

Furthermore, included with this change, would be that the money being earmarked for the Department of Homeland Security (DHS), should be utilized toward re-building moral values and a work ethic in our most vulnerable youth, ages 14-19 through an involuntary draft program. It is my opinion that the future national security of the US may lie within fixing these children.[2] And, it is stated with a high probability that the

---

It is imperative that the United States present a unified front to deal with GWOT issues. Its citizens are the backbone of the country.

[2] While overall public support for a draft is low, support for some type of functional program to help drug users and non-performers in life is high. The Youth Challenge Academies that already exist by the

National Guard has the resources to fix these children, by having increased funding for the Youth Challenge Academies and military boot camps already in place in the states.

Currently these Youth Challenge Programs are exclusively for kids who accept that they have failed at something, and that want to change and re-start their life.  Under this new proposed program, all kids 14-19 who are undisciplined to the point that their parents cannot control them, will begin boot camp immediately, and serve 2.5 years of involuntary service in the US military.

As the 10th Amendment to the Constitution states, each state or territory of the United States has the primary responsibility to prepare for and respond to disasters and emergencies occurring within its borders.  While often overlooked, the tragedy of undisciplined, delinquent, and sinful children is having a direct impact on the national security of our nation, as has been most evident from the anarchists who set fires in Ferguson, Missouri and Baltimore, Maryland in lieu of peaceful protests.

There are many different reactions to these children.  Some people say that their parents just need to discipline them more.  Others state that they need to go to jail.  Finally, some believe that these wayward children need to be given to other parents, as orphans.

When a child gets to be 14-16 years old, many quit listening

---

National Guard are ready to increase the moral values of our nation, but they need increased funding. The young people being served by these Youth Challenge Academies are the likely future individuals who will need welfare and will keep our court systems and hospitals filled up if we do not act. Having a court system that would force young people who get in trouble with the law and/or drop out of high school between the ages of 14-19 to attend these academies, would have a tremendous positive impact on our society, both morally and economically.

to their parents and begin doing what they learn in school by their friends. If their friends smoke marijuana, then most likely they will. They begin to stay overnight with each other. If their friends are having pre-marital sex, then they will too. If their friends are stealing from Wal-Mart, then they will learn to do so too. In a kids desire to grow up and be like others socially, it is amazing what they will do. Many children who have to report to juvenile court, would have never gotten in trouble if they did not have friends that showed them an action. The parents did not teach the action. Society taught the child the action. Therefore, it is my opinion that we, as a society, need to help these children change. Parents have little impact on kids who begin to get in trouble in school. However, a US Marine Corps Drill Instructor in a closed environment on Parris Island, SC can have an impact on a child. It is my opinion that troubled children (ages 14-19) are sent to US Marine Corps boot camp with the intention to change these children into good kids.

The National Guard is specifically separated from Active duty forces under Article 1, Section 8, and Clause 16 of the Constitution, the Militia Act of 1903, and the National Defense Act of 1916. During any emergency, state governors retain authority over their National Guard forces, and can call them to duty to support the state. Furthermore, National Guard soldiers under Title 32 can provide Law Enforcement Support duties, which is different from Active forces acting in the same capacity. Posse Comitatus[3] was written in 1878 in order to protect the people from a strong federal military. The Posse Comitatus Act prohibits federal, state, and local authorities from using Title 10 forces for direct civil law enforcement activities unless through a Congressional or Constitutional Exemption.

[3] The Posse Comitatus Act was passed by Congress on June 18, 1878 at the end of Reconstruction of the Civil War. This law was to limit the powers of the Federal Government in enforcing state laws. However, this law does not preclude using the powers of the military in law enforcement when exigent circumstances exist, such as when the resources of the city and local governments are overburdened.

Posse Comitatus does not apply to National Guard in active duty, or in a Title 32 status, and does not prohibit federal forces from providing humanitarian disaster relief when needed. Therefore, National Guard soldiers under state control can perform their homeland security functions, with no oversight from Congress, which gives the National Guard the homeland security mission to protect each of their perspective borders (if applicable) as the Governor of Texas has elected to do.

The Department of Homeland Security, as it is currently organized, is a Presidential cabinet organization with the responsibility of security of the homeland, including response to national disasters at the federal level. It currently manages about 16 agencies including but not limited to the US Citizenship and Immigration Services, US Customs and Border Protection, Federal Emergency Management Association, US Immigration and Customs Enforcement, Transportation Security Administration, US Coast Guard, National Protection and Programs Directorate, and the US Secret Service.

All of these services can be managed by USNORTHCOM through tasking to the National Guard Bureau and the US Coast Guard through a re-alignment of funding and authorizations from the currently existing Department of Homeland Security. The US Coast Guard should continue to work the largest share of water border protection, especially as it pertains to water. National Guard Bureau, which comprises of both the Air National Guard and the Army National Guard, will continue to take responsibility for the security of space, land borders, and internal security, including cyber security. It would increase its authority by taking over juvenile services in each state and territory from the Departments of Corrections.

Basically, what this re-alignment would entail, is a re-alignment of funding that is currently going to prison systems and correction facilities to take care of juvenile delinquents, being given to the National Guard Bureau and other Armed Services to help re-habilitate these individuals. This money would be used to place these at risk youth under the care and direction of the US military, which would be overseen by a Federal Service Division. The individuals who are in trouble with the law or have failed out of high school, would serve a 2.5 year service obligation to protect their country during this volatile time, and to learn a new skill in a field that is closely suited to their individual skill set, as well as being re-taught moral values. Individuals serving their 2.5 year service obligation in the military can compete to work in hundreds of military fields, after they complete their original boot camp training, advanced infantry training, and military skill training.[4]

Those individuals who are selected for performing work in the Public Works division, can work with Engineers and other crews to help rebuild the already aging infrastructure of roads and bridges throughout the United States.

The best part of this is the current and future cost savings. The organizations listed already exist and will continue to function. However, the $60.9 billion that is paid additionally to the Department of Homeland Security can be recouped through the usage of the already existing US Northern Command, the National Guard Bureau and the US Coast Guard, in a way that would benefit US society and create better citizens for the future, as well as help improve our decaying national infrastructure.[5] And, approximately six ($6) billion that is being

---

[4] In South Korea, all men between the ages of 18-37 must serve in their military. They accept that they are technically still at war at North Korea, and therefore want all their men ready to fight to protect the country. Generally South Korean men elect to report to the military during their 2nd year in college. While South Korean society puts men at war and not women, they still respect the individual rights of women, and women work in just about any other jobs.

[5] In Israel, all citizens go through training in the Israeli Defense Forces at the age of 18, unless given exemptions based on religious, physical, or psychological grounds. All men usually serve for 3 years and all women usually serve for 2 years.

spent to house and feed juvenile delinquents, will be re-apportioned to the National Guard Bureau for usage in changing these individuals mental, physical, and moral state.

## An Argument

The beginning of my argument is this: in current society, we have a whole generation of young people with drug problems and that are involved in criminal activity, and no desire to change, as we are the most giving and forgiving nation in the world. As we look at the individuals who burned buildings in Ferguson, many were just young people who were hired by the machine in Chicago, Illinois, and bused to Ferguson, Missouri to be paid to create chaos. For $13 an hour, many youth burned buildings, destroyed cars, and committed many other felonies, and some were not even endowed with a conscience to know this is wrong.

The irony of this is that many of these children (ages 14-19) are destined to become scientists, lawyers, Senators, Doctors, Internet Technology (IT) professionals, and Military Officers, but will never become anything because they are addicted to the drugs we have allowed to permeate our borders. "Bob" the agenda driven media mogul, has made it his prerogative to sell drugs as the happening thing to kids via the internet and media. However, marijuana, as an example, is known to make people stupid (as a Police Officer I have dealt with individuals on marijuana who do not even know their names or birthday) and are apathetic. We hand out welfare, food stamps, and other free services to drug users and abusers every day. Is it right for us as a nation to overlook these youth to the detriment of their souls, when we could step in and save some of these youth through disciplined training? Is it right to understand up front, that these kids are heading toward welfare and government dependency and do absolutely nothing about it, when through the re-allocation of funds we could teach them discipline and a job skill? What would George Washington, the Father of our Nation have done? "A free people," as George Washington so eloquently put it, "must be able to manage their own affairs so as not to put a burden on the people." Drug addicted people cannot and will not manage their own affairs because of apathy. Therefore, since these drug users and delinquent kids cannot manage their own affairs, they should be burdened with the obligation of service to our nation, for the future benefits that they will be given as they get older.

To start this would be undeniably controversial, and could start protests greater than have been seen in Baltimore, Maryland and Ferguson, Missouri combined. And, up front I will say that there may be a large portion of African American kids that are drafted because they fit under the category of "delinquent" or "drug user" or "high school dropout." If so, I apologize. However, there will be the same drafting of Whites, Indians, Asians, Hispanics, and others. When I went in the Marine Corps, I was told that there was no such thing as black or white people, as we all bled green. That is how we need to start looking at each other. We are not white American's or black Americans or Hispanic American's, but we are American's. And, as such, we have to pull together to prepare for the future, which will include war, famine, terrible storms and earthquakes, drought, and economic devastation. It may not happen this year or next year; but it will happen as it has happened to every organized civilization throughout the world.

As a proposer of the draft system, I understand that there are a lot of questions that will arise.

1. How would we train National Guard soldiers to perform this vast array of services?

National Guard soldiers are already performing these functions. They are trained to perform space security, border security, and other vitally important security services. They also already conduct Juvenile Training Academies, although not on the scale that is being proposed. Inadequacies that exist can be absorbed by bringing on civilian employees of the current Department of Homeland Security, and working with the existing boot camps of other services to help bring on and manage these young people.

2.  Are we truly free if we have a draft?  To begin to answer this, let me ask a question. Is a drug addict truly free? Is a person who can only make a living through theft truly free, and are our citizens impacted through this individual? Are our citizens who are having their home broken into or their stores put on fire truly free? Sometimes, when we talk of freedom of the individual soul, we have to look at the impact that is imposed on others? Is it fair that I can ride a bike in Seoul, South Korea or Berlin, Germany and leave it outside a business unlocked anywhere and it won't be stolen, but if I leave the same bike outside of a McDonald s in Charlotte, NC it will with a 60% probability be stolen? What about my rights and freedoms as a citizen? Through training these kids to perform work and the importance of being honest, we will set them free. A man or woman much smarter than me once said, "Give a man a fish, you feed him for a day. Teach a man to fish, you can feed him for a lifetime." It is time we teach the next generation to fish, and not all of them can learn to do this with a computer. Some will need to work in restaurants and some will build roads. God made us all different, and we cannot all be cyber warriors, as God made some of special ones infantry and US Marines.

3.  What if a person is drafted in the military and wants to leave? They can't. They will be arrested and brought back for long term imprisonment if they do not serve their country in an honorable manner.  They will receive no future benefits from our great nation if they cannot stay and perform their duty. Ultimately, it is my opinion that they should be sent back to the country that their family was originated from, but this will be argued.  Where there is no effort, there is no American. American's try, and when they fail, they try harder.

4.  What if one of these drafted kids tries to commit suicide? From day one, there will be around the clock supervision of these draftees, monitoring their behavior and moods. However, it will be inevitable that some kids will look for every way out of the hard work and discipline that will be instilled in them.  However, for those who stick it out and work hard, they will be given many opportunities to build a life for themselves and their families, and they will have earned benefits from the Veterans Affairs Office and other Veterans benefits that they will be proud of for a long time.  A suicide will unfortunately happen, but with a strict, controlled environment, and monitoring of depression and other suicidal signs, this can be kept to as low of a percentage as when the kids are living on the streets.

5.  What if one of these kids takes a rifle while they are qualifying on the rifle range and shoots a soldier around them or themselves?  Each Platoon will have at least 2 security personnel on hand at all times, monitoring the situation.  In the event a draftee puts another individual's life at risk, it will be dealt with appropriately.

6.  What type of psychological testing will these kids have to see who may have problems being administered forced discipline and training?  All kids will be given an in depth assessment from a licensed Psychologists, and one on one counseling to determine what problems the draftee may be experiencing and to identify coping mechanisms.

**How the Draft Program Would Work:**

Kids, ages 14-19 that are drafted for service, would have to serve a mandatory 2.5 year service obligation for the benefits that they will receive through the United States Government later in life.  This would be no different than what is expected out of youth in Israel or South Korea.  Kids who have a 2.5 grade point average and that are on track to go and succeed in college or join the military on their own, would be exempt from the draft.

Right now, the solution for these "wayward" kids are to let them find themselves, and to stay on the streets until they are put in jail or change.[6]  Under this program, they will begin training immediately to become a US soldier.

It is my personal opinion that no one can break down a man or woman, teach them skills to succeed and survive, and then build them back up better than the US Marine Corps.  We will have to build a training arrangement between the National Guard Bureau and the US Marine Corps to ensure some of these toughest to train soldiers are prepared for the future service of our nation.

And, we need these soldiers and youth to be trained and ready to serve.  It is with a high probability that the following events will happen over the next 20 years:

[6] A Fox News Report dated 28 Feb 2013 showed that the number of individuals (ex-convicts) who were re-arrested and put in prison over a 3 year period (2008-2011) after being released from prison is 43%. Prison overwhelmingly makes criminals only better criminals.

1. There will be a war requiring increasing amounts of young people; larger than the wars of Afghanistan and Iraq.
2. There will be a catastrophic attack within the United States borders that is larger than the attacks on 9/11.
3. Radical Islam will continue to grow and morph, to a point to where IEDs and beheadings become utilized within the US by Islamic extremists.
4. A minimum of (1) nuclear weapon will be set off somewhere in the world by an organization that we likely do not even know has a nuclear capability.
5. Iran, North Korea, India, Pakistan, Russia, Syria, and China will continue increasing supplies of nuclear weapons, and at least one of these countries will sell a nuclear device to a terrorist organization.
6. There will be at least 3 catastrophic storms, earthquakes, or floods within the United States, requiring full activation of our National Guard, and usage of existing Title 10 forces.
7. There will be at least nine riots in the US which require at a minimum a National Guard show of force.
8. United States Prisons, jails, and juvenile detention centers will continue on a guide slope of decreasing moral values, and increasing radicalization of its inhabitants.
9. China will continue to modernize its Army and Navy, including the building of large Cyber Armies.
10. China and Russia will unite forces, and conduct large scale military exercises together.
11. We will have to become involved to protect the people of Africa. We have put this off for a long time, because we don't have assets in Africa. God will not forgive us for continuing to overlook the rapes, murders, and slavery that are taking place in Africa. China has already begun to Police these areas. The US must act also.

To solve these future problems, which I state with a high

probability are going to occur, we need functional and trustworthy individuals to manage our affairs.

Unfortunately, even some of the best US Marine Corps training will be unable to reach the most drug addicted and scarred children. Therefore, we will need to have an even further training organization led by our training partners in South Korea to teach these young people; through discipline, martial arts, and spiritual training to keep them away from drugs, at least for 2 years of their lives. If they choose to return to drugs after a 2 year obligation, it would be on them. However, their service on the borders of South Korea and in other strategic areas would help free up our US Army partners to train for the next large scale conflict.

And, through an intensive psychological vetting process, some of these children are inherently a danger to themselves or to others. Therefore, through these psychological tests, some of these children will be utilized for building projects and farm initiatives to increase our production in the US while helping these young people build a skill. Not all individuals who are drafted will work as soldiers: some will rebuild roads and an aging national infrastructure, work in fields, cut trees, landscape, and perform other tasks to the support of the US government and its citizens.

Ultimately, it is my belief that the US National Guard and the US Coast Guard can protect our borders, support tribal, local, state and federal law enforcement, and prepare lost young people for lives outside of criminal activities and the availability of drugs. The question would come up: why is it important to our nation to improve our moral compass? My answer to this could only be understood by men who understand the history of this great nation: the storms that protected George Washington during his fight for American Independence, the tornado in the Nation's Capital that helped America beat England in the War of 1812, and other manifest destinies that carnal men and women will not understand, and will seek scientific justification for. My premise is that God has his hand on our nation and our security, and that the future of our nation's security is going to depend on an increase in the moral values of our young people, or we will degrade into a survival of the fittest society (criminal and/or communist).[7] It has been stated before that man has evolved from apes, even though apes still exist. After watching the tragedy unfold in Ferguson, Missouri in 2014, I state that there is a higher probability that mankind and the US population is evolving into apes, then that we are evolving from apes. We have gotten to begin to police our own again, and this is an example way for us to fix people before they are too broken to mend.

Many people reading this will state this has no place in consideration for our nation.[8] Science and technology (such as putting camera's everywhere) can outwit the declining moral climate of man's soul. Yeah right. Just like Eugenics was. It is my opinion that we cannot obtain enough technology to combat the decreasing moral climate that is being found in the US, especially among wayward youth ages 14-19.

And, I state with a high degree of probability that this

---

[7] We have seen entire Police Departments taken over by evil people, such as the Robeson County Sheriff's Department in North Carolina which in 2006 had twenty-two (22) Police Officers charged with corruption. And, there were twenty-seven (27) Baltimore City Prison Guards which were involved in smuggling drugs and cell phones for the Black Guerrilla Family gang in 2013, including at least 3 female prison guards who got pregnant by the same evil gangster, and tattooed his name on their neck.

[8] George Washington was one of the first proponents of a national draft, and he once said "it must be laid down as a primary position and the basis of our democratic system, that every citizen who enjoys the protection of a free government owes not only a proportion of his property, but even his personal service to the defense of this nation." Under George Washington, it was a requirement for white males to be part of the militia.

decline of our morality is directly in line with an Operations Order written by the Russian government itself. We are fools to believe that Russia does not plan for the day that the United States no longer exists. They speak freely utilizing terms such as "post America." They today, believe that they as a country are more moral as we are. If true, as Napoleon said, "the moral is to the physical as 3:1." Therefore, if they are more moral than we are, they have 3:1 odds in defeating us. The victor of war is usually on the side with the highest moral values.

I personally believe the following quote was written by Joseph Stalin or one of his staff, and is the basis for Russian planning for the US:

"America is like a healthy body, and its resistance is threefold: its patriotism, its morality, and its spiritual life. If we can undermine these three areas, America will collapse from within."

I believe that Russia has obtained several countries under their control (through use of arms agreements) that are working with them to undermine the patriotism, morality and spiritual life of this country, and that they have swayed our political elections. I believe that we as a military can sit idly by and do nothing about it, or we can recognize that morality is in the highest keepings of the US military and our society, and work to once again instill it in our ranks. As Napoleon Bonaparte once stated, "the moral to the physical is 3 to 1." We are 3 times more likely to win the wars that we have the moral advantage over than those wars that we have no basis to be involved in. We are losing the fight, in my opinion. Furthermore, it is my opinion that the greatest provider of security and security forces within the US, our churches, are being allowed to decay and die away at a time when we need them most. Many of our older churches, where family graveyards have created pride and a since of belonging to communities, are being replaced by urban super churches, many of which are not committed to the word of God or his tenants, and do not have family graveyards, where headstones are engraved with such inscriptions (these are examples) as Daniel Stilmore, USMC, 1945-1972, Died Vietnam, Purple Heart, or Steven Cazilmire, USN, 1929-1944, died unknown location South Pacific, Medal of Honor.

So, with this in mind, and our past as a great indicator of our future, let's look at what the National Guard would need to succeed as it evolves into the National Guard Bureau Department of Homeland Security or (NGBDHS).

The National Guard is the first line of military response to many incidents that occur in the United States. It was the answer to helping citizens of Louisiana and Mississippi recover from Hurricane Katrina in 2005, the citizens of New Jersey recover from Hurricane Sandy in 2012, and the citizens of Ferguson, Missouri recover from rioting in the streets in 2014, and will be there in the future to help citizens of this great nation. The National Guard currently has Civil Support Teams (CST) that help to identify Chemical, Biological, Radiological, or Nuclear (CBRNE) agents for federal, state, and local law enforcement. Furthermore, the weekend warrior stands ready for the call, when he or she must put their lives on the line to protect the citizens of this great nation. The people of the United States trust the National Guard because it is local people who are there to help. The people of the US do not trust the Department of Homeland Security.

However, the National Guard is no better than the soldiers that it is able to employ on the battlefield. To get a soldier prepared for today's war is not an easy or inexpensive task. Our soldiers today must not only be ready to fire a weapon at the ready, but to be seasoned so as not to fire a weapon if another use of force can exist. So, to build this courageous, sympathetic, intelligent, resilient warrior, we need to start at many levels.

1. **Boot camps:** Our military boot camps are the instiller of the soul of our military. When our drill instructors do their jobs right, they provide the force with soldiers who are capable and ready of performing many missions, following orders, and being self-motivated to take care of themselves, their families, and

their communities.  When boot camps fail, they produce soldiers who are marginal at best, not motivated to accomplish, and unfortunately become dead weight when they arrive at the unit.  We need boot camps that excel men and women to become more than they believe they can be.  Marine Corps Boot Camp at Parris Island, SC has always been able to do this.  Therefore, it is my recommendation that we either utilize their facilities as a "draftees" model training for these soldiers, however under the USMC training standards.  Although I believe the National Guard Bureau can manage the Department of Homeland Security, I believe the USMC can save America by taking these hardened youth (ages 16-24) who are not functioning, and making them hardened soldiers.  There is no organization in the world that can change kids better than the USMC on Parris Island, SC.  The territory is ideal for training drafted recruits.


2.  **A Spiritual Base:**  One of the components that I believe the military has recently been overlooking is the teaching of a spiritual base.  While America leaves the understanding of religion up to the family or individual, our wayward 16-24 year olds should be at least given an opportunity to attend worship services during boot camp.  Many have been taught since they were a kid that "God does not exist."  Also, soldiers who are out of boot camp and that serve throughout this great nation should be taught the moral values that this great nation was built on.  For example, "thou shalt not steal."  Even if you don't believe in God or the Bible, what is wrong with being taught basic right from wrong?  Many kids today have parents who are hooked on drugs themselves, and they were never given a chance to know right from wrong.

3.  **A Sense of Belonging:**  In Japan, a man who loses his job does not come home until late at night after others come home so his family is not ashamed.  Today, no one in America is ashamed.  It does not matter what spiritual sin or law that people break, they usually laugh about it.  I found this most

disturbing when I worked as a Police Officer in Fayetteville, NC and I would respond to arrest a shoplifter at Wal-Mart, and the person would make a snide remark like "well they caught me this time." One time I actually had a male who was caught walking out of Wal-Mart with a television make the statement "I had stolen about eighty of them before so I guess it is time I get caught." We need a sense of belonging in America again that can only be given to young people when they feel as if they are a part of something larger than themselves. Kids who are dropping out of school to smoke marijuana deserve a lot better life than "well, it is America and it is their choice." Other countries do not make this mentality. And, many communities say "it is the parents fault." In some cases, it is. But in others, there are kids who are going to public school and are learning how to smoke marijuana and are learning how to disrespect adults. They are not taught that at home, but are taught this by students in the schools they attend. When parents, who are usually behind the curve ball, identify that little Johnny is smoking dope, it is too late and they are sneaking out of a locked house through a window to smoke dope. We, America, are better than this. We, America, can grasp these kids, let them know that they belong to a great society that has historically done great things, and that being a drunk or a dope smoker is not good enough, as men and women died in the Revolutionary War, the Civil War, World War I and II, Korea, Vietnam, Afghanistan, and Iraq for them to live free. If they become a dope smoking loser on welfare, it should be after they have given something of their life, and not before they have contributed anything.

4. **A Sense of Community:** I believe that the individuals who serve in the military must have an ingrained sense of community, to where they believe that the decisions that are made do involve them, and that they are needed. This is currently failing. About 38% of American's today do not even believe that their vote counts in an election, and those elections are rigged. We American's, do not believe our government or its processes are honest, in the country that used to teach other

countries how to have honest elections. 60% of people polled state the first word that comes to mind when they see Hillary Clinton is liar, but yet 38% of people in America would vote for her as President. We need to build ethics back up in our communities, especially among our leaders, so that we can once again believe in society as a whole. I believe that people keep such a high faith in the response of the National Guard because it is hometown individuals who are responding to emergencies, and they know that they do not have something to gain by helping them. People want to know that their vote counts again, and that our government is honest.

5. **Well-Funded With Good Opportunities:** When the National Guard Bureau takes over the functions of the Department of Homeland Security, it will do so with an increased budget and increased opportunities for all. This funding will help individuals to understand that if they do good when they are drafted in the National Guard, that they have a future. For example, many National Guard draftees can go on to become members of the Border Patrol, or to work at the airports under the Transportation Security Agency. Or, if they perform well and prove themselves, they may be able to transfer to another service more of their liking. However, their baseline will be from the strict boot camp that they are forced to endure to teach them life skills, under the joint and combined efforts of the NGB and USMC.

## So, What Would This Look Like:

Any child age 14-19 who is:

- caught with an illegal substance more than once.
- involved in criminal activity (non-motor vehicle related) more than once.
- absent from school for 30 or more days during any school year with no excuse and no desire to attend school.
- fails to follow the reasonable rules set by the child's parents.

would be taken in front of a Juvenile Court (exactly like most communities have today).

A judge would hear from an accuser (usually a Principal, parent, or teacher) and then make a determination if the child can be reformed and stay at home.

In the event that the child cannot be reformed, and further training is needed, then the child will be placed in the custody of the US National Guard Bureaus Boot Camp, and shipped out immediately to begin training.

For some kids, training will be just like intense school, with increasingly hard physical fitness. For other kids, who have the most extreme cases of attention deficit disorder, dyslexia, drug addiction, refusal to conform to military life, and low intelligence quotients, they will have an extended boot camp with one on one counseling and instruction to get them through. Since boot camp for these kids will include up to 6 months of education to complete high school, which is included with boot camp, the initial enlistment will be for 2.5 years.

Once boot camp is completed, and an individual is capable of performing basic soldier skills, then the individuals will be sent to Advanced Infantry Training.

Following advanced infantry training, soldiers will be sent to their basic course to learn the soldier skill that they will work with over the remainder of their service obligation.

Many of these kids will complete their service obligation which includes a high school education before their fellow classmate's complete high school. Many of these individuals will use their GI Bill benefits to go on to college. Some will remain in the military, and make a career out of it. However, no matter what, they must be ready to deploy automatically.

Having these kids complete boot camp and begin a new chapter of their life will help us keep unemployment low, while ensuring that we can face the serious challenges of our National Security. Many of these soldiers will face violent extremists and evolving terrorists which may strike within the heart of the US. Furthermore, nation states are showing impatience with the world economy, and are expanding their militaries, such as Russia with its military sales of advanced Surface to Air Missiles to Iran, and its military expansion into the Ukraine. Many of these intelligent kids will go into Cybersecurity, and will fight battles that are occurring daily against nation states and transnational criminals and terrorists who want to infiltrate our most secure networks and systems. Also, some of these kids will become specialists in the medical field, fighting the outbreak of infectious diseases such as Ebola, which give rise to questions by the national public regarding how safe we are.

The most successful strategy which would keep the safety and security of American citizens, while advancing our national security interests has to involve fixing these kids that are the most vulnerable for the future. America has to lead from the front, and to do so requires determined, focused, and smart young people who have understanding that they are the future of this nation and this planet.

Many of these young kids will perform duty in foreign nations before completion of their term of service. Their service will be utilized to lead international coalitions such as the North American Treaty Organization (NATO) to fight terrorism, aggression, and disease.

Some of these kids will go into the service corps with the Public Works Division, and will perform work in helping to build bridges, roads, and in Agricultural and military arms building roles.

The ability of the nation to have mass production of military equipment, and especially nuclear capable weapons, is important for the future state. Other nations are once again in an arms race to build a military for creating attacks in the future. We must continue to build an armed force that is capable of not only protecting our borders, but the borders of our neighbors.

Nuclear war is possible during the year 2015 and beyond. In the event that the United States has to evolve into a Nuclear War with other nation-states or terrorist elements, then we need to do so with the intention of winning the war. This is not a friendly game that we are involved in. If a country attacks us with nuclear weapons, they are intending not only to kill everyone in the country, but to wipe out future generations.

Russia, has built entire cities underground in the event of such a nuclear attack. For example, Russia has been pursuing construction of a massive underground facility in the Ural Mountains. The underground area is allegedly the size of Washington, DC and has a highway, massive air filtration system, and thousands of workers employed on this project at any given time. Reportedly, there are pre-stocked food, clothing, water, medical supplies, and other items for living an extended amount of time underground. One analyst report states that this is one of about 400 such facilities being built and managed underground in Russia.

China has built an underground facility in Dixia Cheng, which comprises of a bomb shelter with tunnels beneath Beijing. This has since been transformed into a tourist attraction. It was built for the purpose of military defense, and has been called the Underground Great Wall, as it was built for defense from a nuclear war from Russia.

Many conspiracy theorists abound about the capabilities of underground bases throughout the United States and in other North Atlantic Treaty Organization (NATO) countries. I do not know the full context of what has been built in the US. However, we need to keep up with Russia and China, as they are working together, forming an alliance that more than doubles the size of the US military, and their combined military spending is more than double what the United States spends currently.

South Korea, a military force projection platform for the United States, is slowly moving toward the removal of US forces from its soil. While many of the older people who were alive during the Korean War, understand the importance of having the US as an ally on the peninsula to help support stability, many of the younger people see the American's as just unwelcomed guests.  As the generations get older, they forget what costs America gave to protect the freedoms and economic progress of South Korea, which is most evident when looking at North Korea.

The allied Chinese-Russian alliance, could soon become China-Russia- North Korea, as China has economic ties directly to North Korea.  China has now built rail to the borders of North Korea, as if it is signaling it is ready to begin trade with them at any time.


Chapter (17) What Could We Accomplish if We Increased Moral Values?


*President Roosevelt speaking in August 1941, (before Pearl Harbor)  "The President told Molotov (Soviet foreign minister Vyacheslav Molotov) that he visualized the enforced disarmament of our enemies, and, indeed some of our friends after the war; that he thought that the United States, England, Russia, and perhaps China should police the world and enforce disarmament by inspection.  The President said that he visualized Germany, Italy, Japan, France, Czechoslovakia, Rumania, and other nations would not be permitted to have military forces.  He stated the other nations might join the first four mentioned after experience proved they could be trusted."*


While I was living in South Korea, I thought often of those people who were stuck in North Korea waiting to be rescued.  While I ate 3 meals a day, I knew that within 20 miles there were starving kids who were out looking through weeds and grass for something to eat, and drinking water from rivers that were polluted from North Korean industry. Many people in North Korea find calories today from tree bark. It is disturbing. South Koreans are enjoying some of the highest per capita income in the world. However, what is more disturbing, is that the civilized populations of the world allow them to live like this because they are afraid of a dictator, even after we have seen what a dictator can do during World War II. We are the United States of America. We have toppled Saddam Hussein, Adolph Hitler, Benito Mussolini, Manuel Noriega, and more South American drug lords than can be listed. However, today, the so stated Police Officer of the world is hesitating, like we don't know what to do. This has 100% to do with the lack of moral values in this administration, the lack of faith of God, and the lack of understanding that he who is given much, much is expected. China is now having to step up to the plate to become the Police Officer of the world, as is being shown in Africa. Chinese activities in Africa have expanded massively over the last ten years. They are increasingly involved in the anti-piracy operations off Somalia, and hold exercises with Tanzania and provide warships to the Nigerian Navy. Also, China gets about 5% of its oil imports from Sudan. In 2013, South Sudan began fighting a civil war, and China deployed 700 soldiers as part of a peace keeping mission in South Sudan. Also, China has exported to Sudan Chinese made weapon systems in increasing amounts over the last few years. These weapons are cheaper than Western made weapon systems, and the sales are expected to grow over the future years.

While China is expanding its military, and its military's reach, we in the US seem to be stumbling. We, are to use the worst word in a military officers handbook, hesitating. We have no decisive engagement. This is because we have had over the last 20 years a lot of immoral people at the highest places. In the lowest of places there are still dedicated Judeo-Christians praying for peace, equality, justice and truth.

As I got to know more about North Korea and its people, I

became more and more concerned that we are doing nothing to fix this country and its people, and began to pray more that somehow, some way, North Koreans could begin to join together as a unified nation, and create a Revolution to overturn their country and create a formidable Democracy. I know the US is afraid to get involved in the borders of North Korea. However, I wish it could. I am tired of the starving and dying people in North Korea, when we as the world's police officer, with another world's police power (China) even closer, sit idly by and try to wait it out. I even sat down one day and wrote a letter to the North Korean people, although I have never mailed it and don't know who to mail it to. The following is a copy of that letter.

Chapter (18) A Letter to the North Korean People

Dear sir or madam:

I really don't know why I am writing this letter, besides the fact that my soul pours out for you. I have recently lived in Seoul, and saw the happiness of the people there, and the economic stability of a large amount of the population, who walked as free people and did as they pleased. As I walked up the streets in many small South Korean towns, and along the Han River, the people actually looked like some of the happiest I had ever seen in the world; like they had an inner peace to them. Then, I took a trip to the Demilitarized Zone (DMZ), and looked across at a fake town, that had buildings with no floors, and pretend streets with cars. Why in the world would someone build a town, and have no one live in it? Finally, I saw the tunnel that was to be built under the DMZ, and was moved.

I know, as an outsider writing to you, that you will most likely not believe what I am writing. However, what does not lie, are satellites. If you look down on the earth from outer space, you see countries around the world lit up with electricity. Unless you live in Pyongyang, your North Korean streets and alleys at night are most likely without electricity. And, the only people really able to live in Pyongyang are the inner circle of the North Korean government. For those outside of Pyongyang, it is reported there is little infrastructure, and your government has no plans to give you any.

If you looked at a satellite of the world and the nations that allow freedom of media, you would see that almost the entire world, including South Korea, China, Thailand, and Vietnam, allow, their citizens freedom of information and freedom to be able to speak to anyone that they want. However, your government for some reason does not want you to talk to anyone on the other side of the border. The undisputed truth of this is because you would see that the rest of the world is better off economically, spiritually, socially, and technologically, while you remain in a technological base of the 1950's.

The question becomes, what happened? Kim Il-Sung became Supreme Leader of North Korea after the fall of the Japanese rule. Under his command, North Korea became a Socialist Country, with similarities of the Soviet Union. In 1980, after the Soviet Union had cooled its relationship with Kim Il-Sung, he gained complete power over the country. Through the last 3 decades, and 3 separate family leaders, North Korea has remained in almost starvation, except for the rich that serve the Supreme Leader in Pyongyang.

Over the last 35 years, you and your family have begun to believe that starvation and poverty are ways of life. I understand that you are scared, and just want to see tomorrow. I would be scared if I was you too. I see historical movies about how Adolph Hitler killed Jews during World War II, and how tribal kings in Africa kill their people to keep citizens in check. This is called Survival of the Fittest, and when it moves into man, it wipes out the soul of man and their desire for better. They basically give up hope, and become like animals. Sometimes we evolve into ape like beings. I know hundreds of thousands of people are currently being held in North Korean prisons, or have been killed for questioning the government and its wealthy leaders who take advantage of the peasants of the land. If you were to dare question the Supreme Leader of North Korea on a policy, then you could be killed. The US NBC News station on Friday, January 3, 2014 reported an article where Kim Jong Un's uncle, Jang Song Thaek, was stripped naked, thrown into a cage, and was eaten alive by 120 hungry dogs. He was found guilty of "attempting to overthrow the state." You are not stupid to be scared.

There are many stories like this that are designed to take away your belief and hope that things can get better. I want to write you to explain that you have hope; you just don't know it. Your life has been hidden from its need for a savior. You are a human being. You blush because you have emotions, from an amygdale, which is an almond shaped cluster of interconnected structures above the brainstem. This amygdale is a storehouse of emotional memory. Your amygdale, from having lived life with no hope, is basically wiped out. But it can be revived. You can regain it, and once again feel happiness. There is a God that created heaven and earth. He stands ready to help you in your time of need, but you must seek him. I want to teach you how.

As I see the plight of the North Korean people, I see a people of love. I believe that North Korean's are a very loving people, and love their families very much. I saw the borders of your country, and asked myself why you don't just run South and live freely in South Korea. I was quickly told by an expert that you don't do this because your family would be killed, and their dependents would be killed. When I gained an understanding of that, I gained an additional respect for you as a people. You care enough for each other to where you stay in slavery, so your family will live and potentially survive in the future. It is so admirable.

However, you have been doing it for a while now. Your family and their descendants have been enslaved for over 60 years. You work, but have no wealth unless you are in the inner circle of your President. You want to see better for your children than you have, but you don't really believe you can obtain such because there is nothing to give. I am so sorry.

The beginning of wisdom is a fear of God, and the beginning of understanding is acknowledging God exists. There are a lot of things that I am going to tell you that is important; but if you don't ever get this next point, then you will never get the rest. The summation of it all is from John 15:13 which states that "greater love has no one than this: to lay down one's life for his friends." This is the summary of my entire argument to you, and if you cannot get this, then you will never be able to see the importance of possibly dying for the future of your family and your country. Your future generations depend on you standing up to hatred, fear, and injustice. You must fight even if the government calls you a "racist" for fighting against injustice, or a "criminal" for spreading Christianity. You must fight for what is right because the next generation depends on you.

It is my belief that God wants for you to have way more than what you have. I believe he wants you to be free, and to have a choice to know who he is and who his son is. As you look at the sky, you have to wonder where the stars and moon came from. As you look at the sea, you have to wonder who makes the tides ebb and flow. Who created perfect, 24 hour days and years of 365 days? Who made the celestial heavens, and how do the different seasons come about yearly? You probably have many opinions and customs on where it comes from, and I don't want to get into a philosophical argument.

However, I believe in the Bible. The Bible begins to where God (the maker of all things) created the heaven and earth. I believe if you really look at the sky and the earth, and the rotation of the planets and the heavens and the moon, that you will have an understanding that there was a God that created all things. Matter did not just appear, explode, and create the world that we live in. There was an intelligent designer, who is worlds above any mortal man's intelligence and understanding. If you could talk to your friends in South Korea and China, you would discover that a lot of their people have now begun to believe in Judeo-Christianity. According to Wikipedia, 30% of South Koreans are now Judeo-Christians, and I believe it is more because there are churches with large crosses on them throughout South Korea (perhaps as many as in the US). And, according to WordPress, 10.86% of people in China are currently Judeo-Christian, and they are the largest growing body of believers in the world. What I would love to see, is over the next ten years, North Korea to become the largest growing branch of Judeo-Christianity throughout the world. And, it can happen if you believe, and if you spread the word.

Our God, the God of heaven and earth, has in times past motivated men to change their circumstances. For example, when the Israelites were enslaved in Egypt, he inspired Moses to lead his people out of bondage. And, when the United States sought freedom from England, he guided George Washington and his men to defeat an Army and Navy that were professional, twice his size, and better armed and clothed. However, before he began the stirrings of the people to seek freedom and Revolution, he sought the people to seek his word and a relationship with him. He says to seek him first, and all other things will be added to you.

I have limited knowledge of what assets you have available. However, I know you have a mind and an ability to try to understand for yourself. You are an individual with your own capacity to make sense out of this complex world. I want you to try to understand that God created the heavens and the earth, and that he created you. With a faith and belief in God, you can do all things. As stated in Philippians 4:13 in the Bible, "I can do all things through Christ (the Son of God) who strengthens me." This may not make immediate sense, as I as an individual can't do everything through Christ who strengthens me. I can't fly" for example. I understand your doubt. However, God works in mysterious ways you cannot fathom. Whereas you cannot fly, God inspired men to build airplanes which are able to fly you. These same airplanes carry food and bombs and weapons, and would fly to you if we could communicate with you. God can do anything, through the inspiration of the human beings he created. Is the work of God unusually dramatic on a daily basis? The answer is no. God gives water in due time through rain. He provides the ability for us to plant and grow crops. He placed the fish in the ocean, so that we can have food. God created all animals, and made man over them. The Bible states that man was made in God's image.  When God flooded the earth thousands of years ago because of the evil of man, and he saved Noah and his family (because he was not corrupt) he had Noah build a boat.  God did not build the boat for Noah.  However, he gave Noah the inspiration, the materials, the drive, the motivation, and the ability.  He will do the same for you.  God is not going to give you freedom.  However, if you let him, he will give you the inspiration, the materials, the drive, the motivation, and the ability, just like he gives Medical Doctors the knowledge and intelligence to save lives.  The United States of America has been given great blessings from God, and we therefore try to give back from how we have been blessed.  In the Bible in Luke 12:48,  it states "For unto whomsoever much is given, of him shall much be required; and to whom men have committed much , of him they will ask the more."  The US, from this verse is obligated to help those less fortunate than us.  However, I don't know if it will be during the battle or after the battle.  Our Judeo-Christian organizations will come in if you can only free your country, and we will provide food, water, and help you learn to build shelter.  We can go from there.  And, we will pressure the US government and the Chinese government to step in and help with the overthrow of the North Korean government. It is time.

To begin with, let's look for an argument for Revolution. Why would you risk your life to form a new government in North Korea, or one that may even re-unite both Korea's?

1.   **Wealth Disparity**: Kim Jong-Il was the number one personal consumer of cognac in the world, while from one to three million North Korean lower class peasants starved to death from 1994 to 1998.  He had a personal train with 21 cars and a lobster tank, while many were eating grass, tree bark, or

anything else they could get their hands on to try to consume calories not to starve. Kim Jong-uns wealth is in cash and cash equivalents, and he owns all of the real estate in North Korea. A lot of his wealth is believed to be in Chinese banks. He is living as a king while you and your family starve.

2. **North Korean Prison Camps:** The former bodyguard to Kim Jong Il, Lee young-guk, states he was beaten repeatedly while imprisoned in a North Korean prison camp. He states that he was hit by the butt of a rifle, which left him blind in one eye, and lost all but 7 teeth. In the camps, executions of prisoners, even children, are commonplace. Testimony of a former camp guard, Ahn Myong Chol of Camp 22, stated that people were treated as sub-human, and that he gave an account of children in one country that fought over eating a kernel of corn extracted from cow dung. It has also been reported that prisoners were routinely raped, and that in Camp 22 a baby was cooked and served to the prison guard's dogs.

3. **North Korean Information Void:** The government of North Korea does everything it can to keep information about the rest of the world out of the hands of North Korean citizens. Citizens who speak out against this information void are considered traitors, and they are put in internment camps or killed. However, with the internet, Facebook, Twitter and other public media sites, it is becoming increasingly difficult to keep information out of the hands of North Korean citizens. North Korea often fills this information void by publishing their own propaganda to citizens on how everything in North Korea is better than everywhere else in the world, and that people in other countries have it worse than those in North Korea, using no analysis or statistics.

So, what can God do to help you get out of slavery?  What he has given before are men who are able to serve as advisors and help individuals, to help themselves.  For example, when George Washington was fighting the English, he had help from an advisor from France, Marquis de Lafayette, who helped fight for the American Revolutionary War.  In fact, de Lafayette was so trusted by leaders in the US military, that he was given a senior leadership position as a Lieutenant General, leading American troops.  He was an excellent Strategic Planner, especially during the Battle of Yorktown.  At this final battle of the Revolutionary War (Yorktown), his knowledge and experience (as well as a favorable wind from God that kept General Cornwallis's ships out of the area) helped guide the American's to victory, and the beginning of the downfall of the British Empire.  De Lafayette is recognized as a very key and important member of the United States, and his picture hangs in the US Capitol Building, in the very room that Congress works in, as well as a picture of George Washington.  De Lafayette is very important to the history of our nation, and helped guide our fledgling Democracy through war with England.  However, the cost of the US victory was not free.  Many of the soldiers serving in the Continental Army did not even have shoes, and the stories of the American soldiers walking over ice to fight in Princeton, New Jersey at night are heartbreaking.  Our soldiers suffered a lot, many lost limbs and their lives, and the cost of freedom  was high.  It will be high for you too.  But, after your people have your freedom, you will see the immediate growth that occurs in your country.  China has high speed rail ready to come into your country.  South Korea has open highways ready to open up for you to travel South, and your family members in South Korea mourn for the day that you will be re-united.  The world is standing ready to help once you get rid of the city.  As

Sun Tzu stated, give them the cities, and you keep the countryside. You encircle the city, and don't let them out. Starve them and they will surrender. However, thus is the problem statement set. How do we remove the current government out of Pyongyang, and replace it with a legitimate Democratic government elected by the people, without accidentally putting a crook or non-caring person in office, especially one with a finger on a nuclear device? How do we establish both a Senate and Congress in place with representatives from all other your country, to give their opinions and legitimacy to new laws, so that a Dictator does not just rise and make his own laws, or hire his own cronies in a Supreme Court, to just pass laws the way he wants. We have this same problem in America after over 250 years of governing. How do we establish a new court system, with judges and lawyers, who are able to give true justice to the people, and not just bought or blackmailed justice? I don't know. I can give you examples of what other countries have done, but what works best for North Korea is between your people, through thoughtful prayer and a reflection with God in seeking his will.

However, what you have and how you are living is not fair. God can lead you out of this slavery. He has the power and the desire to lift you and your family up out of these circumstances, and to prepare a better way for you. In fact, in Jeremiah 29:11-13 he states in the Bible, "For I know the plans I have for you," declares the Lord, " plans to prosper you and not to harm you, plans to give you hope and a future." You deserve a better life. You deserve more than to live hand to mouth daily, thankful that you did not die today. You deserve to break free of the bonds of slavery that have encompassed you, just as the Jewish people who were enslaved by Egypt for over 400 years did. However, how do we do this? How do we begin to break through enough to make you believe that you can start a Revolution and eventually win a Civil War against your totalitarian government. The problem is the time that you have been enslaved. You need some momentum that has been lost. You lost the initiative because you did not act when your country was first taken over. However, you can destroy the chains that enslave you, just like East Germany did thirty years ago. How do we create Revolution in North Korea, and motivate the smallest of the small to rise up and fight against tyranny, against oppression and suffering? The world is tired of seeing Kim Jong Un taking all of the resources of the land to make himself rich, while leaving the poor to have nothing. George Washington, after the Revolutionary War, was offered to be a King in America, and turned it down. He understood for a nation to be free, it had to be represented by the people, and not just by one greedy man. However, he was a Christian, and was arguably led by his fear of God. Others do not have that conviction, and lead by greed and desire for power.

I am convinced to have Revolution, you have to have a spirit guiding you. At this time, because of the way you have been held down and the lack of initiative, you don't understand that you have this spirit; but it is there. It can be found, if you can begin to believe that God created the heavens and the earth. He created man in his own image, and gave man everything. The first man and woman who lived on the earth were named Adam and Eve, and they had it made. They had food, and water, and lived perfectly contented in the Garden of Eden (suspected to be somewhere in Africa), until such time as Eve became tempted to eat from a tree that she was told not to eat from. When she did this, then God punished them and threw them up out of the Garden of Eden, and introduced man to hard work and women to child birth. We have had to work for what we have ever since.  And, that is where you are.  If you want Revolution in North Korea, you are going to have to work for it.  You are going to possibly have to die for it.

However, God is most with those that follow his rules and his Commandments.  So, to begin with, let me tell you a Commandment you can begin to put to memory:  " To love the Lord your God (the creator) with all of your heart and with all your soul, and with all your strength, and with your entire mind."  Luke 10:27.  If you begin with that, and commit this to memory to begin with, you will have the beginning of a relationship with God.  For, God (your maker) wants you to love him, and he wants you to fear him.  He does not want you to fear any man, but to fear his rules, and to obey his voice.

Revolution is a word that scares both man and governments.  Governments fear the word, as they want to stay operational for the benefit of the few at the top.  Most want to take care of the people at the top of the government, as well as the corporations that feed off these people.  For example, Kim Jong Un is very happy with the current North Korean government, as he has more assets than 99.9% of other people in the world.  He has an estimated $5 billion US in cash reserves, while he manages the most secretive country in the world.  He maintains and grows a collection of some of the most prized luxury goods in the world, when his citizens wonder where they will get something to eat tonight.  He sends slaves to work in other countries, bringing their wealth home to him, to help protect his government.  North Korean slaves are known laborers on Soviet Union building projects.

However, even as I speak of the disparities within your government, I must admit to some disparities in my own.

Although I am very proud of America, we can all see how the top government officials even in our country benefit the most from government, and their friends who own large corporations benefit as well. Therefore, as we establish a new government in your country, I urge you to look deep into the people that you place in positions of authority, as absolute authority corrupts even the most honest of people. You automatically need accountants, and a supported Senate and Congress to keep these people in check, and to watch their work. Every person needs to be held accountable.

So what is different between what is going on in our country and what is going on in yours? We have problems. However, we as individual citizens have rights, and ultimately laws that are designed to take care of me, the small person. We as a country have made mistakes, which cannot be overlooked, and we are not perfect. We have different races in America, and each race feels they are treated unfairly. White people call black people racist, and are tired of hearing "Black Lives Matter," when white people are dying just the same. What if white people went around and screamed "White Lives Matter." It would be considered racist. Black people call white people racist. Hispanic people are treated as only hired labor. Chinese, Koreans and other Asian races are ignored in America.

However, we do not imprison men for no reason, and rarely have we killed individuals opposed to our beliefs. Our First Amendment Rights have been severely trampled on over the last eight years, but we will bounce back. We recognize the importance of all men, women, and nationalities, as most evident by our currently elected President, who is African American. Our country has come a long way, and continues to work hard to make it better. We have no problems putting our own President on trial, as we did with President Bill Clinton when he lied about his affair with Monica Lewinski, and President Richard Nixon, when he lied about his knowledge of Watergate. In our country, the people demand accountability of the people it puts in office. It is expected that former Senator Hillary Clinton will be put on trial for her lying about work at the State Department, and having Top Secret/Secret Compartmentalized Information on her personal computer. After all, if I, a low standing person in the US, had such on my computer I would be charged, as others have in the past. History will tell if America is fair enough to charge and convict an elitist (former Senator and President's wife).

North Korea, is a country run by a Dictator. He does not care for anyone but himself and those people around him who protect him from being overthrown. He uses fear as a tactic, as shown recently when he had his Uncle executed for a dispute. This is the only way that Kim Jong-un can continue to keep power, and will be the way that his successor keeps power. However, you will not be able to put him on trial, until such date as you pull him out of power.

The world is waiting for you to pull him out of power. There are roads and power grids built right to your border. China has built high speed trains and other infrastructure ready to come in, and are prepared and planned to help stabilize your country. However, everyone is left outside because Kim Jong -Un is running the country, possibly with his hand on a nuclear device. Thousands of people could be hurt or killed because Kim Jong-un wants to play with Nuclear weapons. And, if he was to get a nuclear device in the US, we have a policy that we will retaliate. We will blow up everyone in your country. Your chances of freedom and a new life will be destroyed, from the decisions of just your Dictator.  If the Dictator has some special bunker he can hide from our bombs in, we will send in Special Forces Soldiers who will not sleep until he is dead and has his picture and DNA on the television.  We are American's.  Our ingenuity and tracking ability are perpetual.  He will wind up dead on a US Navy Ship, and will be dumped overboard so no memorial can be placed at his burial site.

Look at Osama Bin Laden and how we tracked him for 10 years until the day we could verify by DNA that we killed him. Look at other terrorists.  Look how we deployed troops into Iraq following the World Trade Center bombing.  The US will not stand by and allow ourselves to be bombed, without retaliation. We are the worst wasp's nest that anyone could ever get into. To be frank, by you not taking over your country, and allowing him to continue to run it; and he making a stupid decision to bomb us, you could be signing your own death warrant.  I, personally, as a US citizen do not want this.  Why would you want yourself or your family to die a rapid death because your country has one ignorant leader.  You need to start a revolution today.  There is no time left.  His stupidity could be your death warrant.

However, I agree that there are some details that need to be worked out.  First of all, we need to ensure that the nuclear weapons are secure.  As you begin to take over the country, you need to secure these devices in a manner that no one can get their hands on them.  One rogue individual with a nuclear device could damage all the work and planning that you put into this revolution.  Therefore we need people on the inside who can guarantee security of the nuclear devices, to ensure no nuclear destruction that goes over into South Korea, China or Russia.  You have gotten to gain relationships with members of the military, who can ensure these devices will not be set off or stolen for use on the black market.

Next, we need some communication with  you somehow. The US would support a stable government in North Korea. South Korea has flags on the border, and many of its citizens have family members in North Korea.  They want to see a unified Korea.  China would support a stable government in North Korea.  We all are tired of looking at maps of the world at night to where South Korea is lit up, but North Korea is in the dark.  We want North Korea to come into the 21$^{st}$ century, and to have its children have opportunities like children around the world.  And, we Judeo-Christians are eager to begin teaching the word of God in your country, without the fear of being put in prison or executed.

I really don't think you can be up for this task though, until we help you understand your need for God.   He is with you.  He will lead you, and won't forsake you.  You need insight to where you are going.  You need to have faith that you can gather people with you, and that will fight when the time comes to take back over your country so that you can live free.  You are a strong people, as is evident in the way you fought us in the 1950's.  You are hill fighters, and can control the battle when it is on the ground.

Realistically, it would be great if the Revolution could gain the support of the North Korean military.  I do understand their fear of falling off and away from their own leader, but it may be time for change.  There have been other successful military coups before.  However, it would be a waste to get rid of a Dictator, just to install another Dictator.  What could we do to find these individuals who could start a government without impeding the rights of the citizens they lead.  Ideally, we want a person who does not want power, but that is an influential leader.   My best example is George Washington, who we elected President after he stepped down and turned in his commission as a General in the Revolutionary Army.  However, I really don't have a modern day example of a person like this.  I believe that God will show this leader to the people when the time is right.

Let's look at some historical examples of Revolutions and how they turned out:

**American Revolution:**  The American Revolution occurred between 1765 and 1783, leading to the overthrow of the authority of Great Britain on the American colonies, and the beginning to the United States of America.  During the beginnings of the Revolutionary War, many people remained loyal to the English crown, and at one point it was only estimated that 13% of the American people supported Revolution.  However, its appointed leader, George Washington, who had a profound respect for the manifest destiny of God, understood that he was leading a Revolution that would change the world, and led untrained citizen soldiers through starvation, cold, lack of equipment, lack of training, and other obstacles to defeat General Cornwallis at Yorktown, VA when a "strange wind" kept General Cornwallis' ships from landing.  Most of us American's understand that this was God's will to keep the ships at sea, while the American's defeated Cornwallis' Army on the ground.   During the Revolutionary War, an estimated 25,000-70,000 people died from injuries caused in the war, starvation, hypothermia, and other diseases.  Since the beginning of our country in 1776, we have grown to become an incredible blessed and diverse nation, offering both economic and military aid to many other countries. Foreign aid has been given to a variety of recipients, including North Korea. In the Bible in Luke 12:48, it states "For unto whomsoever much is given, of him shall much be required; and to whom men have committed much , of him they will ask the more."

**French Revolution:**  The French Revolution occurred from 1789-1799, and resulted in the establishment of a secular and democratic republic that became increasingly authoritarian and militaristic.  However the French Revolution had a profound effect on the world political stage, and it helped instigate a rapid decline in world theocracies and absolute monarchies, and replaced them with Democracies and Republics.  Napoleon Bonaparte became the greatest hero of the Revolution through his military campaigns, and future leadership.  16,000 to 40,000 people died in this Revolution.

**Mexican Revolution:**  The Mexican Revolution occurred from 1910-1920, led by Francisco Madero against Porfirio Diaz.  Over time, the Revolution changed from a revolt against the established order to a multi-sided civil war, resulting in a reformation in the order of the Mexican government.  After the war, the representatives established the Mexican Constitution of 1917, and helped form the National Revolutionary Party in 1929.  It is estimated that 6,000-7,000 people died during the Mexican Revolution.

**Russian Revolution:**  The Russian Revolution occurred from March 8, 1917 through November 8, 1917.  It resulted in the abdication of Nicholas II, and the collapse of both the Tsarist autocracy (Imperial and Provisional governments).  It triggered the beginning of the Russian Civil War, and ultimately the beginning of the Russian Soviet Federative Socialist Republic

(SFSR).  The first Russian Constitution was signed in 1918, and in 1922 the Treaty on the Creation of the USSR was signed which ultimately made the country known as the Soviet Union.  It is estimated that over 120,000 citizens died during this war.

There are other examples of Revolutions, but you get the point.  To summarize:

( )  You need to understand your need for the God of all times, to give insight, protection, and understanding.  The world will be praying for you.

( )  We need the nuclear weapons secure.

( )  We need some communication with you.

( )  We need the Revolution, from the beginning to be televised.  If it is televised, and the world sees what is happening, other governments, possibly led by the United Nations, may step in to help.

( )  We need one point of contact, a leader, who we can communicate with and ensure that we know what is going on.

( )  There needs to be an established chain of command.

( )  Guerrilla warfare seems to work best.  Attack large numbers with small groups when they least expect it.  Take their weapons and equipment.

( )  Remember, as Sun Tzu stated, "leadership is a matter of intelligence, trustworthiness, humaneness, courage, and sternness. "  You need all of these things.

Sincerely,

*Tim Trull*

Chapter (19) Protection for our Christian Missionaries

*Sam and Nancy Davis were Christian Missionaries who worked in Mexico. They spread the message of Christ to people in this poor country, and were targeted by the Zetas drug cartel. The Texas couple spent about 90% of their time in Mexico, and had been working, helping people in Mexico for almost 30 years. Why in 2011, after 30 years of working in Mexico, did the criminal organization suddenly feel brave enough to attack American Missionaries?*

There has always been an unsaid law that resonates around American's. "Don't Tread on Us." We are a forgiving people, and one that gives more than we take. However, as we are trampled on we become the most vicious snake that has walked the planets. US Special Forces soldiers can kill people in unimaginable ways, and in a rapidity of pace that is unearthly. However, we have been hesitating, confused between what is right and what is wrong. When Osama Bin Laden bombed our buildings, we set earth and stars aside to find him and finally kill him. We located Saddam Hussein hiding in the earth behind a house. We find our enemies, locate, and destroy them. It is this strength, ferocity, and fear that have paved the way for our Christian missionaries to travel the world and spread the word of God.

When Sam and Nancy Davis died in 2011, the response should have been immediate. The lives of these 2 Christian Missionaries should have been worth the lives of about 100 Las Zetas members. Instead, we did nothing. We hesitated. When we should have seized the initiative, and made a statement, we were eerily quiet, like "you can go out and do missionary work now around the world, but the US government will no longer back you." We are fools. The American government is dependent on God for our blessings. We are dependent on spreading the word of Jesus, and bringing about a better tomorrow by fighting evil around the world. This administration has handicapped our Special Forces soldiers who are trained to take care of situations like this.

There are two primary forces at work in the US today, as in other parts of the world. They are good and evil. Every day that we give the initiative to evil, it begins to override the good that is done. We have lost the initiative, but we can gain it back.

We are the Police Officer of the World. The US has an obligation to protect those weaker than themselves. "Give me your tired, your poor, your huddled masses, yearning to breathe free, the wretched refuse of your teeming shore. Send these, the homeless, tempest-tost to me, I lift my lamp beside the golden door." This is etched on the Statue of Liberty. To those whom much is given, much is expected. At the very top of the George Washington Monument in Washington, DC is a placard on all four sides, that see's the sun before anything else in Washington, DC. It states simply, "Laus Deo," or Praise God.

We are the United States of America. I cannot say it anymore plainly than Charlie Daniels did when he said, "this lady may have stumbled, but she ain't never fell. And if the Russians don't believe that they can all go straight to hell. We are going to put her feet back on the path of righteousness and then, God bless America again."


Chapter (20) Elections

*"When my wife and I voted in the 2012 election, we watched as an African American man and his wife/girlfriend/friend went to the table in front of us and claimed to be a certain person. The lady asked him what his address was. He said he just moved. She said "where do you live now," and he said I cannot remember the address. She then gave them both a ballot and told them to go to a booth and vote."*


What is represented in the White House, on television, and across America is not a true indication of who we are across America. Although it was a television program, go back and look at old episodes of "The West Wing," on television. That is who we are. We are a giving country. We are a country of Blacks, Whites, Hispanics, Asians, and other nationalities that for the most part go out of our way to help others. We have values of right and wrong. There are those on crack and that use drugs and that are just plain mean, that hurt others. But, for the most part, American's today are still who they were ten years ago, with the same beliefs and concerns. We want to raise our children, and for them to have a better life than we have. We want world peace, but will take war if it betters the next generation's way of life. We understand that the best and the brightest Harvard Law School and Yale Law School graduates who are inspired by God should lead us, and not a bunch of liberal fags who would lie about taking the last cookie from the cookie jar. Ethics matter. Lying matters. Truth matters. Justice matters. Hispanic Lives Matter. Black Lives Matter. White Lives matter. Asian lives matter. All Lives Matter.

When we vote again in the future, we need to vote for the brightest, most experienced, most influential, most admired, most educated, most truthful, most God fearing, and most seeking the will of God candidate that is placed before us.

And, we must demand to see identification cards of those who are voting. They had to have an identification card to get welfare, ride a plane, register for a college class, and get financial aid. Why can't they show an identification card to vote. The reason. Because there is a group of people, based out of Chicago, but financed by a wealthy man from Hungary, that wants to put the worst of the worst in government. They believe that if they control Washington, DC, that they can control the US. If through deception and lying our country is taken over by them again, then we are taking the next step toward taking the firearms away from those who need them for protection and to hunt. The criminals and crazy people will not give up their guns. Therefore, I beg our American citizens and hunters who have legitimate firearms to fight this fleecing of America with all of your heart and all of your soul. Our First

Amendment rights have been taken.  We have lost the initiative, and will have to work hard to find honest reporters and news crews to gain it back.   The Second Amendment is next. Remember Nazi Germany.  Weeks before they took the Jewish businesses and properties they went around and took up all the guns.  Through deceptive and lying politicians, that is the next attack.  Don't give up your guns.  It is your Constitutional Right to carry them and to own them.

Chapter (21) Economics

*The income threshold for the United States Supplemental Nutrition Program (SNAP), formerly known as Welfare, is $35,000 a year for a family of five. Each year, approximately 14,000 US citizens on welfare are convicted of welfare fraud, most for felonies, and the average time to be served is 25 years. There are approximately 47 million US citizens who use welfare, and the average income of recipients is $9,000 a year.  These convicted are usually the poorest of the poor.*

Over the last 50 years, the American economy has transformed from one dependent on local businesses, to one dependent on businesses from all over the world.  For example, when I recently had to have my daughters Apple Computer fixed, I had to have a part shipped in from China that had to clear customs at a port in California before I could receive it.  I had to wait 2 weeks for a simple part to fix the computer, because no one in the US could sell the part. The US economics have changed dramatically over the last twenty years, in a fashion that the rich around the world have become richer and the poor have become poorer.  Excessive usury is charged to the poorest of the poor.

Microeconomics continues to be defined by the small user or business.  It basically studies the behavior of individuals and firms in making decisions regarding the allocation of local resources. The primary forces that are involved in this is on supply and demand, and their relationship to price. The amount of a commodity that a person consumes regardless of the price is called its elasticity. Recently, in The State Newspaper, an article discussed an upcoming football game being held in Charlotte, North Carolina between the University of North Carolina Tar-heels and the University of South Carolina-Gamecocks, would have sold 20,000 more seats if they lowered the cost of the tickets. There is an alternative product, television, and people chose to watch television for basically free instead of going to the stadium to watch the game. However, the prices of a NFL Super Bowl game ticket last year at a cost of over $2,000 each ticket. Consumers for a high profile game such as this are willing to pay any price set so far, in order to say they were at the game. Elasticity also includes milk. People usually pay whatever for a gallon of milk, until it gets to a certain price, and then the demand goes down. However, there are products which are blowing the standard economic models out of the water. There are people on welfare who are willing to pay $600 for a new I-Phone, but do not have food in their cabinets and need to use a SNAP card. They look at this as a necessity. When I was at Northeast Junior High School in Charlotte, North Carolina in 1980, I took a Sociology class and I remember the teacher discussing with us the necessities of life. These included at that time food, clothing, and shelter. Since 1980, these necessities have arguably changed to include a car, a cell phone, and a form of identification. It is not uncommon in North Carolina to see a person living in a run-down, broken porch single wide mobile home in North Carolina with a $70,000 Ford Raptor Truck or Mercedes Benz in the driveway. The giving of credit by banks for luxury items is phenomenal. My best friend when I grew up, Brad, was driven around by his dad in a Cadillac. I remember thinking how rich his parents must have been, and I loved to get in the leather seats when I rode with him. Today, everyone owns a Cadillac that wants a Cadillac.

I am not saying the current economic situation in America is right or wrong.  However, I am saying that we are not saving any money, and the poorest of poor are not saving anything.  We are sold to believe that this savior known as the United States government will continue to take care of us when we get old, and in a lifestyle and flexibility of life that is even greater than today although we are no longer producing any real income in the US.  Many of our citizens get on welfare out of high school, and it is like they are raised to become welfare recipients.  People on welfare make out better than people who work at restaurants.  When I first finished high school, I worked at Quincy's Family Steakhouse in Charlotte, NC and got a paycheck of about $250 a week while I was in college.  It covered my apartment, my gas, and my truck payment.  Today, people have cell phone bills they have to cover also, the price of food has gone up, and gas prices have increased.

It seems reasonable to raise the rate of the minimum wage for employees so that they make at least a little more.  But, it also seems to make sense that we cut government payouts on welfare and other benefits to a rate that it is more reasonable for a person to get a job than to become dependent on welfare out of high school.  Our government does not have very dependable people running its books, and it is a shame that our citizens are dependent on a government that's only solution is to keep raising the amount of money it prints each year.  At what point will we have printed so much money to where it creates hyper-inflation, or a serious devaluing of American currency?  Will Social Security and Medicaid survive the next 20 years?

## Conclusion

One Saturday, I was working the 3-11pm shift as a Police Officer.  I was assigned to Zone 23 in Fayetteville, NC which is near Raeford Rd. and Seventy First School Rd.  When I first came on shift that morning, my supervisor told us during our briefing to look out for a stolen, Gold in color Cadillac that was stolen from a local dealership.  When you are on patrol after a supervisor makes a statement like that, every other car it seems is a Gold Cadillac. Anyway, I happened upon a gold color Cadillac turning right onto Raeford Rd. near Seventy First High School. I ran the tag, and it came back as stolen. The driver saw me and quickly did a U-Turn and started heading the other direction. I did a U-Turn also, and the vehicle was going really fast, and out running me as I was more focused on calling it in than catching up to the car at that moment. As I continued up Raeford Rd., I saw people outside of their car on the highway. As I drove up, I saw the Cadillac with the door open, and all the people were pointing toward a church about 300 meters away from the Cadillac. When I looked I just barely saw the suspect run around the corner. I really felt lost as I did not see the car crash, and now I was behind trying to get the suspect, which appeared to be about a 17 year old black male, who ran like Bruce Jenner used to. I drove my car to behind the church and observed the suspect jumping over a fence that has the rolled concertina on the top. I remember thinking "I cannot do that" as I got out of my car and ran toward the fence. When I got to the fence, there was a man and his son inside of the fence, who had a blanket in their car, and before I got to the fence they threw the blanket over the fence, and I was able to get across with my big body and my 15 lbs. of gear (vest, gun, radio, baton, etc.). We Police Officers don't travel light. I kept thinking "what a blessing those two were." I then had to jump over the fence also on the other side. For some reason, I kept running although I could not see the suspect. He was really out running me. On the radio people were screaming, "Bravo-23 where are you." I embarrassingly could not remember the street I was near and just kept trying to describe being behind the storage facility running away from Raeford Rd. I confused every Police Officer in Fayetteville. I was embarrassed, and praying "God help me." I kept running and came into a neighborhood. In the neighborhood this man came driving up in an old, Purple Ford Pinto. I asked him, "did you see a kid running up through here?" He replied, "he was back up the road, get in." I jumped in the Ford Pinto with the man and he drove me right up to where the suspect was. I saw two road signs and called in my location. I remember being amazed at this man's generosity, and wanted to thank him immensely for driving me to the suspect, but the suspect was running again. I was out of the Pinto and I was running again. The suspect jumped the fence into a neighbor's back yard. I barely scaled across the fence, like an old man with 15 pounds of gear on would. The suspect jumped over another fence. I was thinking in my mind, "I am not sure I can do another fence," when this woman came out of nowhere and opened the fence for me. I was running again after the suspect who was gaining on me again. He jumped over another fence. I ran and climbed over the fence, fell on my side, and got up and started chasing the suspect again. I lost my radio. I was running and was now in another person's backyard. I was tired and could barely breathe. I was praying but cannot remember what I was praying, probably something like "Lord help me." The suspect jumped over another fence. I was running toward the fence and wondering if I could climb over the fence. Suddenly, to my right side, came a person running like at Mach speed past me. He slid face first under the fence with his arm, and grabbed the suspect's shoe, as he was now on the other side of the fence. The owner of the fence came over and opened the gate for me. I walked around and handcuffed the suspect and took him into custody. I had lost both my baton and my radio as I continued to jump over fences after the suspect, and citizens brought me both of them. The Officer that grabbed the foot of the suspect was a 23 year old rookie, who later became one of the best Police Officers I have ever seen. The suspect was charged with Felony Possession of a Stolen Motor Vehicle and other crimes, and he led us to a ring that had stolen other cars.

When I think of how we need to Police each other, I think of this miraculous chase, not because of anything that I did, but because of how God lined everything up and how citizens helped me, a Police Officer, catch a criminal. I think of how I, as a Police Officer, could have never had a chance to catch this suspect if it was not for God having these people who had similarly aligned moral values to me help me to accomplish God's will.  God said "thou shalt not steal."  These people helped put a crook behind bars.

As we go forward, it is my sincere desire that we could, as a nation, become a similar unit, in helping put criminals behind bars, in helping to stamp out election fraud, in helping to fix and correct the Internal Revenue Service and other government agencies that are stinking of corruption and improprieties, that we would seek God led people for public office, and that we would remember, that everything we have, everything we are, and everything we will become will only be that way through the blessings and will of a Heavenly Father, who only wants what is best for his children.

Thank you for reading my book.  "May the Lord bless thee and keep thee.  The Lord make his face shine upon thee, and be gracious unto thee.  The Lord lift up his countenance upon thee, and give thee peace.  And they shall put my name upon the children of Israel; and I will bless them. "  Numbers 6:24-27

www.ingramcontent.com/pod-product-compliance
Lightning Source LLC
Chambersburg PA
CBHW060356290526
45791CB00002B/530